Visions of Creation

VISIONS OF CREATION

Edited by
EILEEN CONN
JAMES STEWART

Foreword by
MATTHEW FOX

GODSFIELD PRESS

Copyright © 1995 Godsfield Press Ltd
Text © 1995
First published by Godsfield Press Ltd 1995
Designed and typeset by Sarah Tyzack

ISBN 1 899434 60 7

Write to
GODSFIELD PRESS LTD
Bowland House
off West Street, Alresford
Hants SO24 9AT

The right of the contributors to be identified as authors of their work has been
asserted by them in accordance with the Copyright, Designs and Patents Act 1988

A CIP catalogue record for this book is available from the British Library

Printed and bound in England by Biddles Ltd., Guildford and King's Lynn

To Petra

Contents

PART THREE: THE MODERN QUEST.

About the authors

EILEEN CONN writes and consults freelance on holistic values in action with special interests in corporate spirituality, organisation transformation, business ethics and community relationships. She was formerly a senior civil servant in the UK Government. She is a member of St James's Church community in Piccadilly, London.

MARTIN COUNIHAN is an interdisciplinary scientist and Director of the Centre for Science Communication at the University of Southampton. He has special interests in cosmology and in the history and interpretation of science in context.

JOHN DOYLE lives in Dublin. His background is philosophy and theology, with an MA in creation spirituality, and qualifications in biodynamic psychotherapy, which he now practises. Formerly administrator and teacher at the Centre for Creation Spirituality in London, he is now developing workshops and courses in Ireland.

JOHN FRANCIS GREEN was a school teacher before being called to the ministry in the Church of England. A summer placement at St James's, Piccadilly, introduced him to the Centre for Creation Spirituality. He is now curate in Tadworth, Surrey. A member of the Third Order, he took the name Francis at his ordination.

JEAN HARDY is a writer and teacher. She was a university teacher in applied social studies, sociology and political philosophy. Trained in psychosynthesis, she has written on its spiritual dimension in her book A Psychology of the Soul. She writes articles and pamphlets as a Quaker.

DAVID HASLETT was formerly a senior lecturer in English and drama at the West London Institute of Higher Education. He is now a freelance writer and consultant.

MADELEINE O'CALLAGHAN is a graduate of the Centre for Creation Spirituality in Oakland, California. Formerly a teacher, she is currently Director of The Old Stable House, a spirituality centre in Suffolk, and works internationally as a retreat/workshop leader and spiritual counsellor. She is a member of the Institute of St Louis, a religious community of women.

JAMES STEWART was a senior lecturer at the University of Newcastle upon Tyne, with special interests in 'Theory of Place'. His doctoral research was in the history of relationships between Celtic communities and the land. He teaches and writes freelance in environmental and Celtic studies and Celtic spirituality.

RICHARD WOODS is Associate Professor and Director of the Centre for Religion and Society, at the Institute of Pastoral Studies, Loyola University, Chicago, teaching also at Blackfriars College, Oxford. He is a member of the Dominican Order and has written extensively on the history of spirituality.

EILEEN CONN and JAMES STEWART, the editors, have worked in partnership for several years writing, and offering courses and workshops, both indoors and in the field. The partnership gave birth to this book.

Foreword

MATTHEW FOX

I know a very sincere and committed Protestant minister in the
United States who for years had a Native American as a spiritual
director. Then he started receiving messages from his dreams
that he ought to return to his Celtic spiritual roots. (He was Welsh
by ancestry.) He came to realise that the years he spent doing spiritual practice with native Americans and integrating their spirituality
into his Christian practices (for example around confirmation practices and rites of passage for adolescents), was a kind of preparation
for returning to the Celtic Christian roots of his European ancestors.

I suspect that there is a wisdom and warning in this story for many
of us who are Europeans or European Americans. It follows the
admonition of Carl Jung that we westerners ought not 'to steal
wisdom from foreign shores as if our own culture was an error
outlived'.

This book is a rich one. The reading of it demonstrates that our
culture and religious history was not entirely an error outlived. In
fact, the wisdom that comes through so boldly as the reader advances
from one story to another contains the exact seeds of thought and
renewal for our religious/spiritual imaginations which are demanded
of us today if we are to move from the modern era to the postmodern one. And since post-modernism includes a respect for the
pre-moderns, this book is especially timely for it puts us in touch
again with our pre-modern ancestors: those mystic-prophets who
did not succumb to anthropocentrism or to patriarchal dualisms in
their understanding of religion, but instead saw the sacred in all
creation. This includes the sacred to be found in human creation,

understood as a marvel of spirit and creativity, justice and liberation, forgiveness and knowledge. The individuals celebrated in this book, while they are diverse in personality, gender, cultures, and historical contexts, nevertheless share a common spiritual tradition: that of creation spirituality. And so common themes emerge time and again in their lives and work: themes of panentheism (God in all things and all things in God); of cosmology; of humour; of intelligent use of the intelligence God has given us (including a respect for science and for the investigation of nature); creativity and a respect for the contribution of the artist to religious faith; faith as trust; a sense of goodness, ie., blessing-consciousness; a struggle against narrow and control-oriented ideologies and structures; a passion for justice.

Deliberately short and readable, this book poses a rich introduction to some of the finest wisdom figures of the west. One lesson that comes through strongly is how much we owe to Celtic Christianity. Would we have had a Hildegard of Bingen, a Thomas Aquinas (who was introduced to Aristotle by an Irish professor as a young man at the University of Naples), a Meister Eckhart, a Dante (whose principal mentor studied with Aquinas) or a Julian of Norwich without the Celtic theological tradition? Surely not. How it behoves us today, then, with the ecological crisis looming so large and our religious imagination so undernourished, once again to tap into our rich, Celtic, sources.

In many ways this book presents an affront to fundamentalism. Why? Because fundamentalists are quite unconscious about history. As a result they tend to substitute man-made precepts for the spirit-filled process that has taken place in that alternative Christian tradition known as 'creation spirituality'. As Martin Counihan puts it in Chapter 10, 'Biblical literalism has never been mainstream Christianity'. What is mainstream is the following of Jesus who was both prophet and mystic. Religious renewal means a spiritual renewal and this means the awakening of our energies and possibilities for both mysticism and prophecy. This book, by honouring particular Christians who lived such a spiritual life, invites us all to the banquet. Our ancestors are not meant to be put on pedestals and handily locked away into calendar dates of the ecclesial season, but to be imitated and to be invoked as powers who can intervene on our behalf and send their ancestral courage and imagination our way once again. As Eileen Conn puts it in her excellent summary, this book allows us to reconnect 'with the holistic visions of our ancestors'. Visions are important to awaken the spirit and stretch our souls from the trivial to the grand, from puny-souledness to magnanimity.

Institutional religion, which unfortunately at this time in history is often caught placating the fear-filled fundamentalists rather than challenging us all to spirit-stretching, has much to learn from a book like this. Much in institutional religion in our day is in meltdown and is rotting away. There is much to suggest that institutional religion in the forms (might we say 'wineskins'?) in which we have known it ought to step aside and let the mystical emerge once again. This is inevitable of course. It is already happening. Beauty will triumph over coercion or boredom or forgetfulness, as Dante demonstrates.

Another question raised by this book is the following: can we hope for a sequel? There are so many wonderful creation-centred persons and movements in the west that could not be included in this volume – such as the mysteries of Chartres Cathedral, the tradition of the Green Man, the Goddess, Bede Griffiths, Gerard Manley Hopkins, George Herbert, William Wordsworth, Walt Whitman, John Muir, W.B. Yeats and many others.

My thanks to Petra Griffiths of the Centre for Creation Spirituality and to Rev Donald Reeves, the Rector at St James's, Piccadilly, for their hosting so many creation spirituality events and speakers. And to Eileen Conn and James Stewart for gathering these talks together. How fitting it is that these essays were gathered in the old Celtic lands of Britain. I also thank all the authors in this volume.

With this volume ignorance is being slain. The deconstructing of a religious attitude that ignores spirituality is being accomplished. Thus the healthy reconstructing of religion is afoot. This book provides a fine introduction to awakening our collective memories to visions of creation. Visions that are more alive today than ever, given our new creation story from science and given the peril that our earth-home finds itself in. May these visions inspire many to the action and the contemplation, to the prophecy and the mysticism, that our times demand.

Preface

The book and the vision

This book traces a vision of the earth and the universe through the lives and work of some of the great sages of the west. Nine authors, from England, Ireland, and America, have collaborated to provide an anthology of saints, scholars, poets and scientists from the seventh to the twentieth centuries. The list is by no means complete, and its composition is the result of the enthusiasms and interests of the contributors. Jointly they trace the growth of a great hypothesis of an organic creation which has only begun to be explored scientifically since Darwin and Einstein opened the doors of modern science. But the book carries a further hypothesis, that the vision of an organic world traced through history contains wisdom necessary for us to approach the problems of the twenty-first century. Therefore, there is a hypothesis of perennial wisdom in the book also.

The people who inhabit the following pages are all from the European Christian tradition. This is deliberate, because the materialism of western civilisation has cut it off from its roots. The book addresses the western world, and attempts to offer some snapshots from its own past. But, as the writer says of Thomas Aquinas, thinkers of the stature of the people chosen, as it were, for our camera, belong to humanity. They stand alongside the great sages of every culture. Their wisdom reaches across our petty divisions of nationality, race and religion.

So we offer the book to everyone, to natives of Europe, to those millions of European descent all over the world, to those from else-where who have come to live in Europe, and to all who have been affected by western civilisation. It can be read in sections reflectively or as a whole. It is not intended to be a series of exhaustive studies, but rather a set of short chapters which can be read easily and quickly. Some chapters are biographical, some poetic, some philosophical, and we hope they are inspirational. Each chapter is referenced, and there is a list of books for further reading at the end of the book. Perhaps the short insights will tempt the reader to follow the vision. The vision may inspire renewed hope for the future.

The book is drawn from a series of talks and workshops offered at St James's Church, Piccadilly, London, in 1993. These were arranged by the Centre for Creation Spirituality, based at St. James's. The series was initiated to explore the creation tradition of the west which has often been forgotten. We hope this set of essays will make some of the series available to a wider public. We have worked hard to keep the book small and readable, addressing heart as well as head.

Eileen Conn and James Stewart
London and Newcastle upon Tyne
February 1995

Acknowledgements

First and foremost this book is a joint effort, an anthology of several people's work. The editors gladly record their thanks to the team of authors, who have been highly enthusiastic, patient of our sometimes draconian editing, and completely supportive. What they have written is no mere abstract from their notes for their talks, but carefully worked chapters. So our thanks go to Dr. Martin Counihan for chapters on John Eriugena, Charles Darwin and Teilhard de Chardin; Rev John F. Green for St Francis of Assisi; Fr Richard Woods OP for the chapter on Thomas Aquinas; John Doyle for his work on Meister Eckhart; Dr Jean Hardy for thoughts on Dante's Divine Comedy; Sister Madeleine O'Callaghan for her window into the world of Dame Julian of Norwich; and David Haslett for his revelations in the world of the poets. The writers all have busy teaching, writing, and professional positions, and letters have crossed the Irish Sea, the Atlantic and the English Channel as we have exchanged drafts with them.

We especially acknowledge the work of Petra Griffiths at the Centre for Creation Spirituality, in designing the series of talks and encouraging us in our attempts to make the material available to a wider public. Our thanks also go to all the workers at the Centre, mostly volunteers. We are grateful to Rev Donald Reeves and St James's Church for hosting so many creation spirituality events over the years.

Debbie Thorpe, partner in Hunt and Thorpe, our publishers, encouraged us from the first mention of the enterprise, and has stayed with us through changes in her publishing policy. We want to record our thanks to her for support which was essential to keeping the team of authors going, and for her tolerance of us.

Several friends who became aware of what we were up to were

enthusiastically supportive. We thank them all, and particularly Keith Murray, Marianna Koeppelmann and Alison Temple.

Last but not least, we thank Matthew Fox for agreeing to write a foreword within a busy international lecturing schedule. The inspiration of the lectures he has given at St James's provided some of the energy for this book, especially his call to those of us in Britain to look to our roots, the wonderful insights of our Celtic and Anglian ancestors. We hope he will enjoy knowing that some of the work was done in Cuthbert's Northumbria. So we also acknowledge the inspiration given by the people of old who handed down the vision, without whom this book would never have been written.

Copyrights

For particular permission we thank Thomas Kinsella for his translation of the poem in Chapter 2, from the *New Oxford Book of Irish Verse,* Oxford University Press; Bear and Company of Santa Fe for quotations from Hildegard of Bingen's *Book of Divine Works*; the Society of St. Francis for the verses from the *Canticle of the Sun,* and Oxford University Press, New York, for quotations from R.D. Sorrell's *St Francis of Assisi and Nature;* Element Books for the quotations from *Meister Eckhart: Sermons and Treatises*; and Paulist Press for quotations from Hildegard of Bingen's *Scivias,* from *Meister Eckhart: The Essential Sermons, Commentaries, Treatises and Defence,* and from Julian of Norwich's *Showings.*

We wish to acknowledge all the other authors whose works have been briefly quoted or referred to in the text and in the notes and references. These include works out of copyright, and the writings of sages and authors of long ago so essential to this book.

We have worked within the recommendations of the British Publishers' Association and Society of Authors' copyright guidelines, but if we have inadvertently overlooked anyone we hope we will have used their work appropriately and that they will accept our thanks.

Eileen Conn
James Stewart

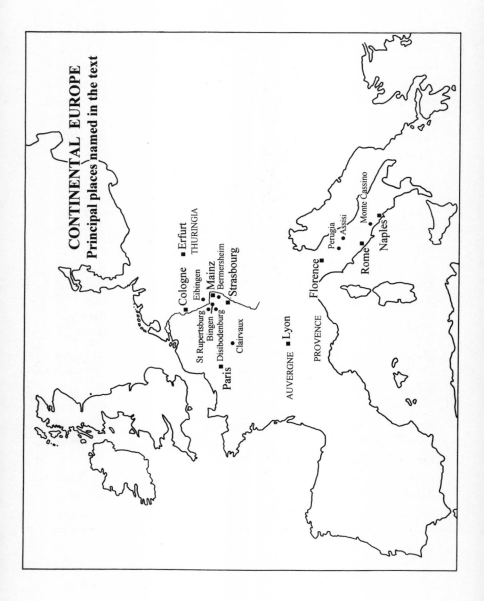

CONTINENTAL EUROPE
Principal places named in the text

Cologne
Erfurt
THURINGIA
Eibingen
Mainz
Bermersheim
St Rupertsburg
Bingen
Strasbourg
Disibodenburg
Clairvaux
Paris
AUVERGNE
Lyon
PROVENCE
Florence
Perugia
Assisi
Monte Cassino
Rome
Naples

THE BRITISH ISLES
Principal places named in the text

Iona

Firth of Forth

Abercorn
St Abbs
Lindisfarne
Farne Islands
Old Melrose
Bamburgh
Coquet Island
Chester -le-Street
Tynemouth
Durham
Hartlepool
Solway Firth
CUMBRIA
Whitby
Ripon
DEIRA
York
Humber

Derry

Armagh

IRELAND

MERCIA

Tipperary

WALES

Norwich

Oxford

London

Canterbury

Bockhampton

Prologue

Visions of life

JAMES STEWART

There are more things in Heaven and Earth, Horatio,
Than are dreamt of in your philosophy.
WILLIAM SHAKESPEARE: *HAMLET*

Go outside, when the stars are shining, and look out into that deep velvet darkness. Find the thin tracery of light like a belt of shining dust across the sky, the Milky Way, and you are looking across the spinning disk of your own galaxy, out into history. The light from some of the most distant stars in our galaxy has taken many millennia to reach us. We have not yet discovered the edge of the great universe of which our galaxy is a tiny part. Signals from the farthest stars we can detect can take up to six thousand million years to reach us at the speed of light. The actual stars have moved on from where they appear today. Indeed they are so far off they can only be detected as radio signals. You are looking at the shifting dust of a great cosmic explosion that happened billions of years ago. We are all specks of that dust, stardust! We are part of what we see out there.

Look at the flowers, the grass and grain of the fields, the great trees that will outlive you. Turn over a stone, and see scuttling away a host of tiny creatures. Look at the sparrows on the rooftops, the birds of the garden, the dogs and cats of the city streets, the wildlife of the countryside. See the children next door, the people around you, the families pushing the supermarket trollies loaded with food for the week. What is going on all around you? Life! Something which began on this earth maybe three billion years ago in the hot waters and volcanoes of the early oceans. We are all part of that life.

WORLD-VIEWS OF THE WEST

This book is about the lives and work of some people who have shared a very ancient, and at the same time a very modern vision. It is an organic and holistic vision; organic because it is a vision of a living universe, holistic because the universe is much more than the sum of its parts, it is a whole interdependent entity. The magnificence and intricacy of the starry heavens is also present in the flowers at our feet, and in the atoms and molecules in our own bodies. Holism is more than seeing the whole. Each particle contains the imprint of the greater reality. There is a web of relationship from the smallest particle of matter to the universe itself.

This was remarkably well understood by our ancestors, and is being rediscovered by modern science. The earth, including humans, is a complex 'living system',[1] a great web of life. We cannot separate ourselves from nature. What we do to nature we do to ourselves. In the lives and work of the people in this little book there is a sense that humanity and nature, matter and spirit, are so interwoven that they cannot be separated. This view of the world is deeply embedded within the history of Christianity itself. The 'west' has its roots in mysticism. Often this has been forgotten or deliberately denied. But it is a dynamic vision which was frequently at odds with religious institutions which had become frozen within rigid doctrines. It is a highly spiritual vision of life.

Another ancient view of life is the 'dualistic' idea. It is a separatist concept, dividing the spiritual from the material realms, soul from body, gods from humans. It always accompanies the desire for power; power over nature, over the earth's resources, over others. It also allows us to split ourselves in two, the subjective me from the rational me, the religious me from the secular me, I the kindly neighbour or member of a human family from I the ruthless boss.

The major modern alternatives to the organic and holistic worldviews are mechanistic and reductionist ideas of creation. These see the universe as a great machine, a 'majestic clockwork',[2] which can be understood by reduction to its basic parts, by taking everything to bits. Maybe we can understand a clock or most pieces of machinery this way, but once we do this to living organisms they are no longer alive, and we certainly cannot put them together again!

The machine idea changes our relationship to the world, as we become observers, analysts, managers, seeing and operating from outside nature. So this is a dualistic model *par excellence*. It has been a foundation idea of western philosophy since René Descartes (1596-1650) defined the Earth and the universe as a machine, a concept which he and Francis Bacon (1561-1626) extended logically to include all living organisms and the human body itself.[3] Descartes also asserted that only what could be shown to exist without any doubt could be accepted as reality,[4] including his own existence: 'Cogito ergo sum', I think therefore I am!

Machines have, of course, been used for centuries. They are extensions of human potential for doing work. But ancient civilisations did not transfer the idea of the machine to the creation around them. Yet, paradoxically, reductionist science and machine technology have produced the methods and equipment needed to rediscover complexity in nature far beyond any clockwork, however majestic. The world is mysterious again.

A BRIEF JOURNEY THROUGH TIME

This book is a pilgrimage through time. Each chapter is a snapshot of history. We start in northern Europe, in the chaos between the fall of the Roman Empire and the rise of medieval civilisation, surrounded by turmoil, tribalism, migration and conquest. South of the Alps the early Roman Church sought to keep some grip on classical civilisation. At each stage of history there was turbulence. Europe has not been a peaceful place. There was suspicion between the Roman church and the less rigidly organised northern Celts. In medieval Europe we find similar mistrust between the mystics and the dogmatists within the church. Many deeper thinkers were declared heretics. But as George Bernard Shaw said in his play *Annajanska,* 'All great truths begin as blasphemies'. Sometimes these are old truths that have been driven underground. This is not just a religious issue: it affects all who challenge accepted norms in society.

Copernicus (1473-1543), Kepler (1571-1630) and Galileo (1564-1642) between them proved that the earth was not the hub of the universe. They introduced a new cosmology, a new world-view based upon scientific theory and observation. The furore which followed was because the church, on the authority of divine revelation, had taught that the earth, and humanity, were the focus of divine attention and the centre around which the universe revolved. Ecclesiastical anxiety was felt across Europe, but the Roman church especially saw itself as God's agent on earth. Galileo shot away a major prop for the authority of the church. The response was that of the police state, to try to silence the heretic.[5] Several popes had vested much in a struggle for power over the previous centuries, battling against the Holy Roman emperor in the middle ages for supremacy. In the sixteenth century the struggle turned to resisting the Protestant Reformation. The move away from belief based upon divine revelation to understanding based upon scientific proof opened the door for the Enlightenment. Henceforth human intelligence would conquer all the mysteries of nature through objective detached observation and analysis.

The book does not include a chapter on a particular person from the Enlightenment. But it is important to say something about this period of western history, because most of the dominant attitudes and values of the modern industrialised world were developed between the sixteenth and mid-nineteenth centuries in Europe. The problems of life would be solved by human ingenuity. Newtonian physics provided the basis for the real age of the machine, and the industrial revolution. Nature herself became a resource for human exploitation and curiosity. The essence of the age was a search for certainty. This included a certainty in religion; certainty of our origins, of individual salvation, and of the literal truth of the scriptures. So Archbishop Ussher (1581-1656) by adding up the ages of the patriarchs in the Bible, calculated that the world began on 23 October 4004 BC. The Cartesian desire for proof affected every walk of life. The great machine of the universe was itself proof of the existence of a designer, God.

In the early Renaissance we still see the idea of the complete human being. The skills of all the arts and sciences were cultivated to their full within the individual. It was the age of 'Universal Man' (*sic*). The best known example is Leonardo da Vinci (1452-1519). But as the range of knowledge increased it became impossible for anyone to be competent in more than a small area of skill. Specialisation became a necessity. Science became separate from the arts, engineering from architecture. Human learning became fragmented. Religous life became separated from secular life. For many the new scientific age was the pathway to atheism; God was an unnecessary hypothesis.

In such a setting the role of the mystic passed to the poets and artists. They were free to re-possess the old office of the bard, and to keep alive the deeper truths. Several religious mystics also arose, even in the Protestant north. John Donne (1572-1631) reminded people that 'No man is an island'. John Bunyan (1628-1688) wrote his *The Pilgrim's Progress*, the English answer to Dante's *Divine Comedy*, the soul's journey. George Fox (1624-1691), the father of the Quakers, preached the 'inner light', reflecting the 'divine spark' of Meister Eckhart.

The role and position of women changed during the medieval period. Women enjoyed high status in Celtic and probably in Teutonic cultures. The Irish myths in particular illustrate this.[6] In the Celtic church the abbesses enjoyed a role which came from a long cultural tradition in society. The gradual suppression of women can be traced as the Roman tradition replaced the Celtic and Anglian,[7] but outside the church the position of women in society was also changing as the age of feudalism progressed. Between the women in the stories of Cuthbert, and Hildegard of Bingen, something had changed. Simeon of Durham[8] tells of the turmoil when married clergy were no longer permitted to serve in the church and women were excluded from much of Durham Cathedral, being denied access to the shrine of St Cuthbert. By the fourteenth century Dame Julian of Norwich had to tread a careful path between her role as a visionary anchoress and counsellor, and her position as a woman in the church, but her visions of Divine Love have never been surpassed.

CONNECTING WITH OUR ANCESTORS

It is not easy to relate to the great visionaries of the past. They lived in a world we cannot enter, and thought in ways often quite different from ours. Our ideas of reality are not the same as theirs, as they had not travelled the long road through history which separates us from them. They speak a different language in which religion, science and art intertwine in ways less common today. Their lives are wrapped in ancient myths.

The role of myths in society has largely been forgotten. Myths are carriers of truths and values. Since the nineteenth century history has been about facts, gleaned from records of the past analysed with scientific rigour. But ancient historians were concerned with pointing a moral, extolling a nation or its heroes, and conserving tribal or national norms. So the lives of early saints and heroes are interwoven with miracles and wonders. These indicate the ideal characteristics that great people of the time should possess. So we relate to our ancestors on several levels. First, we can glean a great deal about the life and character of the 'real person'. Then from records of what they wrote or said, we can understand something of their message to the world of their day. From the mythology that has grown around them we can glimpse how they matched up to the standards of their time. We get a sense of their personality, their vision, their world, and how they experienced life and its meanings.

But we cannot escape from our own world. We see these people through the window of our own age which, like modern stained glass, carries the icons of today. None of these people could possibly have imagined life in the late twentieth century. We, likewise, have no experience of their world, nor could we survive in it very long. They could not speak to us directly. We eavesdrop on voices from another age, rather like indistinct radio signals which we try to hear against a whole mush of interference. How well we can tune in depends on our skill as receivers.

Ancient people are the ancestors of all cultures, as much our relatives as our own parents and grandparents, the creators of so many of the ideas and values still cherished today. The organic vision of the world is rooted in the ideas and attitudes of tribal forebears, formed by their closeness to and direct dependency on nature. Most European value systems, philosophies and religious practices were created in the middle ages, but these incorporated elements of classical, Germanic, and Celtic pagan philosophy and customs. Modern western science is the product of the last four centuries. But the way Thomas Aquinas and other scholars began to apply rational argument to theological problems in the thirteenth and fourteenth centuries prepared the ground for the full rebirth of rationalism in the fifteenth. Life progresses like a rich tapestry. The living are the latest threads in the design, and they cannot see where the pattern is going.

What we can see in this tapestry is a vision of the universe, a perennial wisdom, that is timeless. There are deep values that are shared across the human family, transcending race and religion. These we can translate into our own language and apply in our own day. The qualities of goodness and compassion that add up to saintliness are still true. The defects that are visible in past societies are still part of the human condition. The sense of our place in nature, the essential sanctity of the earth, and the way we endanger our own existence if we forget this, are clear messages for our day.

But this is not a history book. It is a book of visions, conveyed to us by nine different writers of the modern age. Each writer has established their own relationship with their subject. To this intricate pattern the reader brings his or her own vision. Also, we can at any time we choose go out and look at the same stars which our ancestors gazed upon, and wonder. We create our own visions, and our own myths, every day. In a sense, every scientific theory is a new myth, every religious idea a new legend. We weave myths around our own friendships, around our own life stories, and we believe in them.

THE POST-MODERN VISION

In 1859 Charles Darwin came crashing into the apparent certainties of Victorian England. Landing heavily on the library tables of the western world came his great thesis *On the Origin of Species*. It showed that the world had not been stable since it came into being. Millions of years of evolution lay beneath our feet. Humanity was not created whole from the dust of the earth in a garden six thousand years ago, but had evolved over millennia along with every other creature. There was not even a directing hand. Darwin was followed by Einstein, and the concepts of relativity and quantum theory, and then by the new cosmology and the 'big bang'. Certainty, and absolute objectivity, were banished. Once again the religious world saw its certainties vanish, and science and religion entered another age of conflict. But Darwin, like Galileo, could not be silenced.

The effects of these discoveries are just being understood in the last decades of the twentieth century. A new world-view is emerging, a new myth, much closer to the medieval organic vision than to the machine model of the scientific age before Darwin and Einstein. The Gaia theory explains the earth as one great living organism. Maybe we now feel closer to Francis of Assisi than to René Descartes. Maybe Meister Eckhart's 'God within' is much nearer our spiritual experience than the remote deity of the Age of Reason. The poets took up the inevitable lament for the loss of innocence which Darwin's great work brought upon us. Then, as a new battle was engaged between religion and science, new prophets also arose, prepared to grasp the wonder of this new cosmology and to discover a new spiritual experience of reality. The universe was becoming mysterious again. Humanity could begin to recover its sense of its place and role in the evolving creation. A new vision of life is coming into being. New myths weave themselves into the tapestry of human experience, and the pattern grows richer.

THE MYTH OF THE TREE

A mythical image runs through most great religious traditions: the Tree of Life. In the Christian tradition it re-appears at the end of time in the midst of the heavenly city, where its leaves were for the healing of the nations.[9] It figures in Celtic art. Charles Darwin used it to describe the ascent of humanity.

Imagine a great tree planted on the earth, its roots reaching under every continent, carrying the sap of many ancient cultures to feed the tree. The roots are all very similar, although the ground is often very different. The roots feed the green leaves, which are for our healing. We must care for the roots or the tree will die. The roots are often covered up by the concrete of civilisation. This book is about some roots which grew in Europe, but the tree fills the earth. It belongs to all humanity. Our vision of creation is central to our survival. 'Where there is no vision, the people perish.'[10]

PART ONE

The Celtic Way

1

Compassion and community:
Cuthbert of Lindisfarne
(635-687)

James Stewart

It is the 31st of August, AD 651. High in the Lammermuir Hills in south east Scotland, a young man pulls his cloak about him as he watches over his master's sheep. Away to the east is the cold North Sea, with the Island of Lindisfarne lying in sight of the Royal Citadel of Bamburgh, capital of Northumbria. Near Bamburgh, sheltered by a rough tent, a Celtic monk leans, dying, against the walls of a small wooden church. Sixteen years earlier he had left Iona, in the Hebridean Islands off the west coast of Scotland, to bring Celtic Christianity to Northumbria. Sent for by King Oswald, in 635 he founded a simple monastery on a bleak little island on the edge of the stormy North Sea. Tonight he will die an exile, a 'white martyr'. Suddenly the young man watching the sheep sees a strange light in the great northern sky, descending to the east, and ascending again like a band of angels carrying a shining soul into heaven. Cuthbert the young shepherd is witnessing the passing of St Aidan, the first Celtic bishop of Lindisfarne. As morning dawns Cuthbert sets out on a journey that will end three and a half centuries later when his body is finally laid to rest in Durham Cathedral.

CUTHBERT

Cuthbert's life is probably the best recorded of any of the early British saints.[1] He was born around 635, and died in 687. He became a Celtic monk, although he has an Anglian name and was brought up by a foster mother called Coenswith, probably in Lauderdale. Fostering was a custom of the Celtic aristocracy, so that children of the ruling houses would grow up in the community, experiencing the life of the ordinary people. He was an athletic child. In 651 after his vision of the death of St Aidan he presented himself as a candidate at the Celtic monastery at Old Melrose on the River Tweed three miles east of modern Melrose. He arrived at the gate on horseback, lance in hand, with his attendant by his side. Like many then entering the monastic life he was probably from a noble family. He studied under Prior Boisil, succeeding him in office. During this time he also served for a short interlude as guest master at Ripon in Yorkshire. In 664 he went to Lindisfarne as prior.

Cuthbert had a deep desire for solitude. At Lindisfarne he would retire to a tiny island now called St Cuthbert's Isle, just offshore. Eventually he withdrew to the Farne Islands, but even there he was visited regularly by the Lindisfarne brothers, and princes and important church people from all over England came to seek his counsel. He built himself a deep enclosure surrounded by a high wall, that allowed him to see only the starry heavens. In it he built two huts, a house and an oratory. Near his landing place he built a small guest house for visitors. Solitude was not isolation, and his sense of community embraced all who wished to see him. He was more or less dragged back to Lindisfarne in 684 to become bishop. When he felt his health failing he went back to his hermitage to die, pleading to be buried in his hut for fear that his body would become a focus for pilgrimage if it was taken back to Lindisfarne for burial. His brothers persuaded him to change his mind, and his relics have been visited by millions of pilgrims and visitors ever since, at first on Lindisfarne, and later at his final resting place in Durham cathedral. He became a saint for all England, and patron saint of King Alfred the Great.

Scandinavian raiders harrassed the east coast of Britain during the eighth and ninth centuries. In 875 the Danes carried out a massive raid on Northumbria. Eardulf, sixteenth bishop, exhumed Cuthbert, along with the remaining bones of St Aidan, King Oswald's head and the relics of bishops Eadbert, Eadfrid and Aethelwold. With these and the beautiful Lindisfarne Gospels Eardulf and the community fled to the Solway Firth, intending to sail to Ireland. They were prevented by a storm, and after wandering across northern England they settled at Chester-le-Street in County Durham. In 995 further raids sent the Community of St Cuthbert, as it was now called, to Ripon for a few months, after which they travelled north again. But Cuthbert's cart refused to move past Durham, and a final resting place was found on the Dun Holm in the great loop of the River Wear where the Norman cathedral now stands. Cuthbert's pilgrimage was ended.

THE CELTIC COMMUNITIES

The Lindisfarne community was a daughter of the Community of St. Columba at Iona. Other communities following the Celtic tradition on the east coast included Abercorn in West Lothian, St Abbs or Coldingham in Berwickshire, Coquet Island and Tynemouth in Northumberland, Hartlepool in Durham, and Whitby in Yorkshire. Lindisfarne lies about half way along this string of monasteries, lamps along the shore of a war torn Britain. At the same time Anglian settlers appear to have been establishing new villages into what is now south east Scotland.[2]

Celtic society was based upon the family, and upon the tribe which was a group of related families. Rights depended not upon charters and contracts, but upon relationships. Each tribe was a self-contained entity, although in confederacy from time to time with others. The Celtic monasteries were established within this tribal tradition. They had emerged very early in Ireland in such profusion that some think they may have been Druidic colleges which had accepted early Christianity.[3] The monasteries could be male, female, or twin houses of monks and nuns usually under an abbess. Buildings were simple round huts enclosed by a ditch and wall, with a small oratory or chapel. In Northumbria they were of timber and thatch. The monasteries were not like the rich medieval establishments with which we are familiar, but more like communities of hermits, living very ascetic lives. Nevertheless they were important centres of learning and medicine. Each house had its Rule, usually based on older models such as those of St Columba or St David.[4] Columba's rule divided the day into prayers, work, and reading. Work was of three kinds: personal work, work within the monastic community, and work in the wider community of the surrounding countryside. The monks also were deeply aware of their place in the whole community of nature. In Cuthbert we see all these inter-related aspects of life lived out, in individual life, in the shared life of his close friends and colleagues, in the countryside and its people, in his visits to other monastic houses far afield, and in his closeness to other creatures of creation.

· Bishops were pastors, teachers, and missionaries, subject to the abbot or abbess. They wore ordinary monks' dress, and there was no territorial diocesan system. But it was not only the bishops who wandered the wild countryside preaching and healing the sick. Many ordinary monks went out across Britain and Europe on missionary pilgrimage. The idea of 'The Journey' is built into ancient Celtic mythology, and it emerges in the 'white martyrdom' of the exile for Christ. Most Christians understand the 'red martyrdom' of a violent death for the faith, but the Celtic church also recognised 'white martyrdom' in the permanent forsaking of home, family and normal life to take up a wandering existence as missionaries and scholars. Going wherever their calling took them, their community was the whole world.

In continental Europe a different tradition was emerging, salvaged from the ruins of the Roman Empire. European monasticism evolved from the example set by St Benedict (480-547) at Monte Cassino. Emphasis was on the withdrawn enclosed community, increasingly dedicated to scholarship. Monks were not to wander but to stay in their communities. The political power vacuum in Rome was filled by the ascendancy of the popes from the sixth century onwards. Pope Gregory the Great, a Roman civil servant turned monk, began to apply the methods and laws of the Roman Empire to the growing church.[5] In 597 he sent Augustine to Canterbury. Augustine landed at Thanet, and founded a monastery at Canterbury alongside the ruined ancient church of St Martin, thirty-four years after Columba founded Iona.[6] Augustine proposed the division of England into twelve dioceses, which the British church resisted. From Canterbury, Paulinus took Christianity to York, where King Edwin of Deira was converted. But Edwin was killed in battle and Paulinus retreated, leaving the north open to the Iona missionaries. But the Celtic and Roman traditions were to clash in Northumbria the very year Cuthbert became prior of Lindisfarne.

THE SYNOD OF WHITBY

In 664 the Synod of Whitby met to decide whether the Celtic or Roman tradition should prevail in Britain. Hilda, a grand niece of King Edwin, was abbess of the twin monastery of monks and nuns at Streaneshalch, on the headland south of Whitby harbour. She was given the veil by Aidan himself. Supporting the Celtic church at the Synod were King Oswy, Colman the Irish Bishop of Lindisfarne, Bishop Cedd, and Abbess Hilda and her monks and nuns. The Roman case was supported by Oswy's son Prince Alfrid, Abbott Wilfrid, Bishop Agilbert of the West Saxons, and the priests Agatho and James.

There were differences of practice between the two churches. The loose federalism of the Celtic churches and monasteries contrasted with the Roman diocesan structure. The Benedictine Rule was not generally established in the Celtic church. The Roman tonsure was not worn. The Celts calculated different dates for Easter. The monasteries were independent centres for wandering missionaries, rather than enclosed houses under standard rules. But the theological debate hinged on the Celts observing the Rule of Columba and holding St John as the leading apostle of the Church, and the Roman church's appeal to the authority of St Peter vested in the pope. Colman argued the Celtic, and Wilfrid the Roman case. King Oswy accepted the Roman argument. Colman and his monks retreated to Iona. The decision affected the whole network of Celtic monasteries across northern England and southern Scotland. Whitby was the beginning of a long process of change in the north, from 664 to 1068. What evolved in Northumbria was an Anglo-Celtic church under the authority of Rome, but retaining much of Celtic spirituality and way of life.

CUTHBERT IN THE COMMUNITY

From his early days at Melrose to his death Cuthbert had a deep sense of the importance of the community and of every individual in it. At Melrose he was caught in a plague which decimated the monastery, and in caring for the sick he became ill himself. The brothers prayed all night for his recovery, and when he learned of this in the morning he insisted on getting up and resuming his ministrations. As a result he retained a weakness for the rest of his life. He gave himself totally to the community in which he lived.

Cuthbert succeeded Boisil as prior of Melrose. They spent the last week of Boisil's life going through the Gospel of St John. A mystical gospel, it starts with the assertion that divine light is present in everyone from birth. The closeness of John to Jesus and his theme of human and spiritual love appealed to the Celts. Bede in his Life of St Cuthbert recounts how Boisil and Cuthbert dealt only with the 'faith that worketh by love', and not 'deep matters of dispute'. Celtic spirituality is highly experiential and practical. It is filled with a sense of a spiritual presence in creation and in every person. The Synod of Whitby was won on 'deep matters of dispute'. That is not the Celtic way. Whitby was not set to a Celtic agenda.

Cuthbert went to Lindisfarne to become prior. He was a tender and considerate confessor, his own tears flowing before those of the penitent. He was a spiritual healer, and 'sins' were failures common to all, which like wounds needed healing. He went for nights without sleep, working, praying, and watching, sometimes touring the island to make sure all was well with the community. In the countryside he sat in the villages, gathering crowds around him to teach them.

Cuthbert himself never gave up the Celtic life style. He accepted the decision at Whitby in the interests of church unity, but the members of his community at Lindisfarne had to accept it for themselves. He sat in long debate gently trying to persuade the monks to his view, often insulted by his opponents. He would adjourn the sessions when there was no point in going on, but would raise the issues again, seeking to mediate and persuade. Yet he maintained a cheerful equanimity, radiating gentleness, and quiet joy. His attitude to community is summed up in his own words:

> Always keep peace and divine charity amongst yourselves; and when necessity compels you to take counsel about your affairs, see to it most earnestly that you are unanimous in your counsels. But also have mutual agreement with other servants of Christ and do not despise those of the household of faith who come to you for the sake of hospitality, but see that you receive such, keep them, and send them away with friendly kindness, by no means thinking yourselves better than others who are your fellows in the same faith and manner of life.[7]

Cuthbert's sense of community extended through the numerous monasteries in Scotland and the north of England. He visited them regularly, and seems to have been especially close to several of the great abbesses of his day. He visited and counselled Abbess Aebbe at Coldingham, with her twin house of monks and nuns on St Abb's Head. The trust placed in him is shown by Abbess Aelflaed of Coquet Island, on the Northumberland coast. When she was seriously ill she said: 'Would that I had something belonging to my Cuthbert! I know well and believingly trust in God that I should speedily be healed.'[8] Cuthbert sent her his linen girdle which she put on and was healed. These journeys were often hazardous, and sometimes Cuthbert was sustained miraculously on his travels. For example, when he visited Abercorn on the Firth of Forth, he and his companions, stormbound, were fed with dolphin flesh miraculously prepared for cooking on the beach. He sailed far south to Whitby to see Abbess Elfleda, and to Tynemouth to visit Abbess Verca not long before his death. Verca gave him a length of linen, which he kept for his burial 'for love of Abbess Verca who gave it to me'. He was placed in a sarcophagus given him by Cedd.

We have the picture of a greatly loved counsellor. What is outstanding, in view of later attempts to paint him as a woman hater, is the way in which the abbesses treasured his friendship. Celtic and Anglian society gave women a high status that was later denied them by the medieval church. In the Celtic tribes women could inherit the headship of the tribe in their own right. There was nothing unusual in the seventh century about the great Celtic and Anglian abbesses' status.

Cuthbert's healing stories bring us face to face with the miraculous. Many of these miracles were performed for people in the surrounding countryside. He healed two men's wives at a distance. Sending his girdle to Aelflaed was an example of healing through secondary contact. During the plague at Melrose, he undertook hours of difficult and dangerous practical nursing. A truly gifted healer reaches beyond the boundaries of mechanistic medical care, often leading to a mythical reputation. Miracles may often be normal events experienced with special spiritual awareness. Physical and spiritual health were one and the same issue for Cuthbert. He had a sense of people as whole beings, body, mind and spirit, and of the community as a living sharing organism.

CUTHBERT AND NATURE

Cuthbert's sense of the natural world was acute, and foreshadows that of Francis of Assisi. It reminds us that Celtic spirituality evolved among a rural tribal people, close to and dependent upon nature. Mediterranean Christianity had become urbanised very early, and most of St Paul's letters were to urban Christians, although his letter to the Galatians is to a Celtic tribe in Asia Minor. 'Paganism' is literally the religion of the country people. Celtic 'nature theology' had suggestions of pantheism which alarmed the Roman church.

There are several stories about Cuthbert's communion with other ceatures, but a few must suffice. Once when on his travels from Melrose, without food, Cuthbert spotted a white tailed eagle and prophesied that it would provide a meal for himself and his boy companion. The bird dived towards the river, and Cuthbert sent the boy ahead who came back with a salmon. Cuthbert gently reprimanded him for not leaving half for the eagle and sent him back with the fisherman's portion. Sharing was not just to be between humans, but between all creatures. At St Abb's he was watched immersing himself in the sea all night, and being followed ashore by two sea otters who dried and warmed his feet. On Inner Farne he scolded

the birds for stealing his barley, and they never robbed him again.
Two ravens were caught stealing straw from his roof, and later came
back to apologise and brought him two pieces of lard to grease his
boots. He made friends with the eider ducks which are still known
locally as Cubbie Ducks.

Today most of us have lost this affinity with the natural world.
Cuthbert was not separated from nature by artificial technical and
commercial interfaces. We are all part of the natural system, but are
we aware of it? Survival depends on that level of awareness. The
whole of life depends on green leaves!

CUTHBERT THE SEER

Cuthbert was a seer, sensing things going on in the world beyond
what was immediately obvious. Twice he thought himself visited by
angels. The most remarkable occasion was on a cold winter day
while he was guest master at Ripon when a stranger called. Cuthbert
welcomed him and went to the bakery for bread. He returned to
find the visitor gone, and three fresh white loaves warm on the table.
Looking outside, he saw no one, and there were no footprints in the
snow! He saw the death of Abbess Aelflaed's servant, and the death
of King Ecgfrid at Nechtansmere, while far from the events. His
powers of prognosis were strong. We see a man of acute sensitivity
for whom the material and spiritual were one. 'Heaven' was not
beyond, it was present in the here and now. This sense of the unity
of the material and the spiritual is essentially Celtic. It induces a
powerful respect for all living things. A world managed on this
dimension would be a very different world from ours.

He practised the deep asceticism typical of most Celtic saints.
They were able to let go of material things. Although there was a
hint of Gnosticism, the idea that the flesh has to be suppressed and
that reality exists only in the spiritual realm, there were humane
priorities which modern society has lost sight of, and which are
necessary for our humanity. He brings us a deep sense of the oneness
of human and natural communities, the value of every individual to
the whole organism. His Celtic sense of 'the presence' was strong.
Lindisfarne is an empty place of sea and sky. A place where the early

saints had so little but wanted nothing; a place for letting go! At his final resting place in Durham the Normans erected a huge cathedral over the simple saint. He was painted as a woman-hating priest, a judger of transgressors, and women were excluded from a large part of the church. But on his beloved Lindisfarne we can sense his closeness to nature and the spiritual dimension of life. We can find again a spirituality which we have lost, which we need for our survival and the survival of this planet.

Cuthbert's spiritual path

Cuthbert was one of those who for all time shine in the darkness and cannot be extinguished, having no material ambition, the fools of God. For Cuthbert the negative experiences of life, along with the positive, were necessary for creativity and transformation. After Whitby he turned defeat into a creative energy which fired the English church for four centuries. His sense of the wholeness of everything, his positive befriending of life, helped him to accept the way of darkness, and out of this to create something new and transcendent. He carried the Celtic spirit into the emerging Anglian tradition. His was a 'faith that worketh by love'. Cuthbert's legacy of compassion for the human community and for creation could be the basis of a creativity so needed in the crises of our late twentieth century.

2

A Celtic cosmology:
Rediscovering John Eriugena
(820 -870)

MARTIN COUNIHAN

ohn Eriugena, sometimes known as John Scotus, lived in the
ninth century and was the outstanding spiritual and intellectual
figure of the West during what later, unjustly, came to be called
the Dark Ages. He is an unfamiliar figure to us today largely because
he was reduced to historical obscurity as a result of opposition to a
number of his ideas during the centuries after his death. His name
became associated with heretical tendencies and with alleged
pantheism. Nevertheless he had a deep influence on the modern
world through radical thinkers of the late Middle Ages such as John
Eckhart and Nicholas Cusanus who prefigured Europe's
Renaissance. Rediscovered today, John Eriugena's ideas seem
refreshing and surprisingly relevant. He presents a creation-based
cosmology with a holistic view of nature and of humanity's place in
it.[1]

John Eriugena was born somewhere in Ireland around the year
820. We do not know his 'real' name, because John (Johannes) is not
Irish but is a Latin name that he would have adopted when he
entered the monastic world. Eriugena is a confected Greek word that
he chose, simply meaning Irish-born. We therefore know nothing
about his family and tribal roots.

As a young man John Eriugena travelled to what is now France, and it was there that his productive life was spent. He was never to return to Ireland, but it is possible that he spent the final few years of his life in England. He probably left Ireland about the year 846, when the High-King Niall Caille mac Aeda died and was succeeded by Maelsechnaill mac Maele Ruanaid. Niall, a northerner and the king of Ailech, near the modern city of Derry, had been a bitter opponent of Feidlimid mac Crimthainn, the King of Cashel, near Tipperary in the south. Niall and Feidlimid had for years supported rival candidates for the Abbacy of Armagh, Ireland's prime ecclesiastical position. Feidlimid, in his opposition to Niall, repeatedly sacked monasteries that were under northern control, including the leading centre at Clonmacnois on the Shannon. Meanwhile the Vikings were periodically raiding and ravaging the country: Niall's ecclesiastical protégé as Abbot of Armagh, Forindán, was captured by the Vikings in 845 and ransomed a year later. In 845, too, the shrine of Patrick was broken up and carried off by the Vikings, inflicting a deep cultural shock on the Irish of Eriugena's generation. Incidentally, Forindán's rival as Abbot was Diarmaid ua Tigernain, described in the Annals of Ulster at his death in 852 as 'the wisest of all the teachers of Europe'. We may speculate as to whether Diarmaid was among Eriugena's teachers.

It is easy to see why Eriugena and many like him found it natural to take their loyalty to the Holy Roman Emperor. The Empire had plenty of imperfections, but by comparison with Ireland it was an enlightened and effective integration of political with spiritual unity. For John Eriugena it was to be personified in Charles le Chauve, Charles the Bald, Emperor of the West and patron of learning.

John Eriugena spent his career in the region of Laôn, Compiègne and Quierzy a little to the east of where Paris now stands. He became a central figure in the circle of scholars and teachers surrounding Charles the Bald, then King of the Franks, who became his patron and friend. John Eriugena was a teacher, a Greek scholar and translator, and a writer. To call him a philosopher, or a scientist, or a theologian, or a cosmologist, would be misleading because these are narrow modern categories. He was all those things and more. He entered enthusiastically into the world of theological debate and controversy, and was especially attracted by the thinking of the Greek Fathers of the Church, some of whose writings he translated into Latin for the first time.

REASON, WHOLENESS AND UNITY

To understand the creative spirituality of John Eriugena we should look first at the intellectual tradition from which he arose. That tradition can be traced back to the edge of prehistory, and it consisted of three strands in particular. One was reason, i.e. an emphasis on the importance of individual human thought and an awareness of our closeness to the mind of God. In this respect the early Irish Christians found an affinity with Greek Christianity and with the teachings of the ancient Greek philosophers, and particularly Plato. They believed that all things are contained in the Divine Mind,[2] even ideas have reality, and our duty is to battle tirelessly against ignorance and stupidity.[3]

The second strand of Irish spirituality was to do with the integrity and wholeness of nature. There was a strong resistance to the sort of dualistic views that separated the universe into intrinsically good and evil sections, or built a wall between the heavens and the Earth. The integral, holistic view of nature combined with divinity is resonant with what we commonly think of as 'Celtic' nature-spirituality:

> I am wind on sea
> I am wave in storm
> I am sea sound
> and seven horned stag
> I am hawk on cliff
> a drop of dew in the sun
> a fair flower
> a boar for valour
> I am salmon in pool
> lake on plain
> a hill with ditches
> a word of art
> a piercing point
>   that pours out rage
> the god who fashions
>   fire in the head ... [4]

Thirdly, the concept of catholic orthodoxy was deeply rooted in the Celtic tradition. This can be hard to appreciate today. The word has modern connotations suggesting antiquarianism, dogmatic inflexibility and intolerance. But 'orthodoxy' is a positive belief about the nature of the church as an inclusive community from which nobody should cut themselves off, within which progress depends on the free but structured interchange of ideas. St John Chrysostom, the Greek Christian thinker (c354-407), said that in early Christian Britain people discussed the interpretation of scripture 'with differing voices, but not with differing belief'.[5] Differences of opinion were acceptable, and vigorous debate performed a positive function in the development of the church. We can link the Irish tradition of orthodoxy embracing different views with a broader and more ancient Celtic appreciation of individual imagination, creative tension in argument, and diversity within unity.

The concept of a higher orthodoxy, in the sense that mundane diversity and conflict must be ultimately transcended by unity at some higher level, has its parallels in the political structure of early Ireland. Even in pre-Christian times, across the 'Celtic' West, druidical authority and training were organised across tribal boundaries. In Ireland, in spite of a high degree of cultural unity across the island, there was a patchwork of petty-kingdoms churning in loose alliances, with military and political power coalescing only occasionally and ephemerally around different leaders from this province or that. John Eriugena was acutely aware of the tragic consequences of violent discord between factions of the Christian Irish; and part of his cultural background was the idealised concept of a sacred high-kingship that might bring to the political world the same unity of purpose that could be found in the church at its best. The high-kingship of Ireland was not a political reality, but it was an ideal, contrasting wth a shabby and disappointing actuality in Eriugena's time.

PREDESTINATION AND OTHER CONTROVERSIES

In the mid-ninth century there arose a heated controversy about predestination. The pious idea that God pre-plans everything can lead to the despairing conclusion that human effort changes nothing, and free will is an illusion. John Eriugena, then at the start of his career in France, was asked for his views on the question. He firmly took the view that human effort is significant. He argued that we should not ask if God predestines the future, because God is beyond the dimension of time. For that matter God is also beyond space, so we should not ask where God is either. Heaven, God's abode, is nowhere – a disturbing notion that Eriugena was to develop later in the *Periphyseon*. Space and time together are part of God's creation. God cuts across space-time. Consequently free will is no illusion, human effort is important, creativity is important, and what humans create, God creates. Humanity 'is a certain intellectual concept formed eternally in the Mind of God'.[6] Reasoning, and the building up of knowledge, are holy. 'There is no worse death than ignorance of the truth'.[7]

So there is a hard edge to John Eriugena's spirituality. It is not just a matter of admiring the perfection of God's creation in the environment around us, it is the command to participate in creation as best we can through our own messy and imperfect efforts. We are God's creative agents. This is not something to draw cosy reassurance from. It involves uncertainty, tension, swimming against the tide, the risk of faith, and alienation.

John Eriugena was also involved in debates about the nature of the Eucharist, and on this topic he again took up a radical and distinctive stance: '…spiritually we sacrifice Him; and intellectually – by mind, not by tooth! – we consume Him'.[8] So, while not denying the mystery and reality of Christ's presence in the Eucharist, Eriugena insists that the consumption of the host is intellectual rather than alimentary in character.

THE *PERIPHYSEON* –
ON THE DIVISION OF NATURE

About the year 867 John Eriugena composed his major original work, the *Periphyseon,* in which he presents an integrated philosophy of God, humanity and the universe. It is written in the tradition of teaching and learning through debate, structured as an imaginary dialogue of questions between a Master and a Disciple. Others who used the format of dialogue to introduce controversial ideas include

Plato, Galileo and Thomas More. Eriugena's *Periphyseon* has suffered from suppression and inaccessibility, and it is a long and difficult work. Only recently has a satisfactory and complete English translation been published[9] and it extends to over seven hundred pages.

In the *Periphyseon* Eriugena takes creativity as the fundamental basis of his analysis. Periphyseon is at root a Greek word, meaning 'about nature'. Nature, to Eriugena, is everything and includes God: God is natural, not supernatural! The book has an alternative Latin title, *De Divisione Naturae,* 'On the division of nature'. Eriugena divides nature into what creates and what does not create. He also splits it into what is created and what is not created. He divides nature into four parts:

1   Nature which is not created but creates (God as Alpha)
2   Nature which is created and also creates (Divine Causation)
3   Nature which is created but does not create (Matter)
4   Nature which is not created and does not create (God as Omega)

This double division of nature evokes an image which would have been very familiar to John Eriugena: the simplest Celtic cross, the circle of nature divided horizontally and vertically into four, the same as the astronomical and astrological symbol for the Earth.

The division of nature, on the basis of four aspects of creativity, is the most original feature of the *Periphyseon*. It defines the plan of the book itself, dealing with the four divisions in successive sections. But exactly what are Eriugena's four creative divisions of nature? The first of them, the uncreated creator, is by definition God, the alpha, the first cause of everything. The last, which neither creates nor is created, is also God, but seen as the ultimate objective, the Omega point, and the end of the creative process. Of course, as John Eriugena makes clear, God is beyond the flow of time and it is just to simplify our own understanding that we might distinguish between God as cosmic origin and God as cosmic destiny. Both are the same to God. So, two of the four divisions of nature are simply different aspects, Janus-like, of the same God. Looking backwards and forwards in time, they remind us of Eriugena's time-transcending resolution of the predestination question.

The Celtic Cross as the Circle of Nature

Eriugena's other two divisions of nature are the two parts of the created world: the part that does not itself create, and the part that does create. The latter, the division of nature which is created and also creates in turn, is a difficult concept to describe. It is something like the ideals of Plato, or the angelic orders, intermediaries through which divine creativity stamps itself on the material world. They are sometimes called the 'primordial causes'. For Eriugena they are things like goodness, life, truth, justice, peace, health, and innumerable other things in a similar vein. One might say that these are abstract virtues, or even illusions, but Eriugena considered them to be real parts of the division of nature. Nowadays do we say that scientific laws, for example, are real things? Are the rules of geometry really written in nature, or are they just in our minds? John

Eriugena's answer was that all these creative creations, perceptions of the human mind, are real and natural.

The division of nature which is created but does not create is just the material world around us, which itself is formed of the four elements of earth, air, fire and water. Eriugena devised an original model of the material universe which perhaps owes something to ancient Celtic traditions of reverence for the sun. He places the sun in the central position in the universe, mid-way between the surface of the Earth and the stars. According to him, most of the planets (Mercury, Venus, Mars and Jupiter) orbit the sun. He sees seven equal intervals measuring out the universe, intervals between the eight points of a musical octave. This is Eriugena's vision of cosmic harmony and symmetry.

It can be claimed with some justice that Eriugena anticipated the Copernican revolution. Seven hundred years after him the Polish cleric Nicolaus Copernicus revolutionised cosmology by arguing mathematically that the sun is at the centre of our universe and the earth rotates around it and spins. Although Eriugena was not a mathematical astronomer, and his sun is not stationary, and his earth does not move like that of Copernicus, nevertheless Eriugena was a 'Copernican' in a philosophical sense because sixteenth-century Copernicanism was as much as anything a cultural revolution about the status of humanity and the Earth, and a rejection of cosmic dualism. Thus Eriugena pictures the sun in a prominent, central position in the universe. He does not regard the earth as the lowest of places and the most distant from God, as it came to be seen by the Aristotelian philosophers of the later pre-Copernican Middle Ages. Eriugena sees no need for a geographical hell or heaven. There is no supernatural region, because all is part of nature. This cosmology is entirely consistent with Eriugena's moral theology: there is no physical reality to the Devil, evil is simply an absence of good, and sin has its source in the will of the individual. He says:

> I think you have not yet quite grasped the fact that God
> punishes no nature created by Him, whether human or
> demonic; but that He punishes what He has not created,
> i.e. the irrational motions of the perverse will.[10]

GOD IN NATURE

We sometimes think that the spirit of modern science emerged only at the time of the Renaissance, if not later. But John Eriugena more than a thousand years ago was teaching that the exercise of the free, creative intellect is central to human fulfilment. Living in violent, superstitious and irrational times he attached supreme importance to reason and the logical contemplation of the natural world.

Eriugena dispelled the supernatural, seeing God as integral to nature. His fourfold division of nature formed a sequence of causation: from God as Alpha there emanate creative forces which allow the material world to be ultimately consummated in God as Omega. But while we perceive a sequence from past times towards the future, God is beyond time, because time itself is a creation of God. Space is likewise a divine creation, and God cannot be restricted to a location within it. Eriugena therefore saw no place for a heaven in the naive sense of a geographically-located abode of God. By the same token, he saw no place for hell. However, Eriugena's philosophy demolishes heaven by integrating God into the world, almost to the point of pantheism, rather than by marginalising God or questioning his existence as Newton and Darwin later did.

The key point is that, for John Eriugena, nature and supernature are not separate. Not that he disbelieved in God: but he believed that God is here anyway, manifest in the orderly workings of the natural world and in human reason:

> The cause and creative nature of all things is, and is wise, and lives.[11]

PART TWO

Medieval Insights

3

The interconnected universe:
Hildegard of Bingen
(1098-1179)

EILEEN CONN

Hildegard was born in 1098 in Bermersheim, near Alzey south west of Mainz, the tenth child of Hildebert and Mechthilde, members of the local nobility. They were friends of the Count of Spanheim, whose daughter Jutta decided to become an anchoress. Hildegard was eight years old at the time, and her parents offered her to God by placing her with Jutta. They were enclosed in a cell beside the Benedictine monastery at nearby Disibodenberg. St Disibod had been a Celtic bishop who had travelled from Ireland and settled at this spot in the seventh century, around the time of the growth of Lindisfarne. Over the following centuries there had been a series of Christian settlements around the hill, which overlooked the junction of two tributaries to the River Rhine flowing a few miles further north. In 1105, a reformed Benedictine monastery was established on the site.

Here the young Hildegard came to live with Jutta. She learned to read the Latin Bible and the monastic cycle of prayers and chants. During those early years, when the monastery was being rebuilt around them, other young women came to join them, because of their spreading fame. So their life gradually changed from that of enclosed anchoresses to members of a Benedictine convent, and when she was fifteen Hildegard became a Benedictine nun.

Little more is heard of her until she was thirty eight years old in 1136, when Jutta died and Hildegard was elected in her place as abbess. Five years later, she had a vision which led her to write her first famous work *Scivias,* with the editorial help of Volmar, a monk from the Disibodenberg monastery. *Scivias* took ten years to write, during which Hildegard's fame increased and more women came to join the convent. In a vision Hildegard was told to leave Disibodenberg with her sisters to found a new community. Building on the new site was completed in 1150, and Hildegard and some twenty other nuns travelled the day's journey downstream to St Rupertsberg, near the Rhine.

Hildegard then embarked on the very active and public second half of her long life. As the abbess of the St Rupertsberg convent, she became known as a visionary, writer, preacher, musician, painter, and healer and counsellor to people of all kinds. She produced three major visionary books: *Scivias* (Know The Ways) illustrated by paintings of her visions, *Liber Vitae Meritorum* (Book of Life's Merits), and *Liber Divinorum Operum* (Book of Divine Works). In parallel she was writing holistically about science and medicine: *Physica* (Natural History) and *Causae et Curae* (Causes and Cures), and composing her music and songs.[1]

In her sixties and seventies, Hildegard journeyed hundreds of miles following the river routes from St Rupertsberg, and preaching in public and to the clergy. Sometime around 1165, she founded a second community at Eibingen, a few miles to the north east of Rupertsberg across the Rhine, which she visited twice a week. In 1173 she was just completing her last major book, *Liber Divinorum Operum,* when Volmar died. He was succeeded by other monks,[2] first Gottfried from Disibodenberg, and then Guibert of Gembloux who was with her until she died on 17 September 1178.

HILDEGARD AND AUTHORITY

For a medieval woman Hildegard had a remarkable relationship with the authorities of her day. Popes, bishops, abbots, members of the laity and religious orders, emperors, kings and titled nobility across a wide area of Europe sought her views and advice on a range of matters. These included questions of theology, salvation, church organisation and monastic discipline. This was a time of active questioning about the appropriate form of spiritual life, whether to withdraw more from worldly affairs, or to become more immersed in the needs of the growing urban population. Hildegard took the line of moderation, advising against withdrawal and encouraging her enquirers to persevere with the work they had been called to do. She was also deeply concerned that the clergy were becoming too interested in wealth and power. At the same time there was a deep schism in the church over the respective powers of popes and emperors. This led to decades of localised civil war in Germany during much of Hildegard's life. Against this background, Hildegard's letters are full of forthright admonitions to the highest through to the lowest in church and state to mend their ways.

On several occasions Hildegard found herself in conflict with her church superiors. The most well known include her decision to move her convent from Disibodenberg to Rupertsberg; her opposition to her close friend and fellow nun, Richardis, leaving to become abbess at another convent; and the burial of a man who had once been excommunicated. These conflicts show the tenacity with which Hildegard worked to achieve what she thought was right, and that she was not cowed by having to deal with the powerful, most of whom were men. Her move to Rupertsberg would have lessened the constraints on her activities from the Disibodenberg male heirarchy. Her determination, and the vigour with which she fought her case with the clergy, seems to have been in many cases associated with recurring illness and the onset of a vision.

HILDEGARD'S VISIONS

She first had a visionary experience when she was five years old, and continued to have them throughout her life. Jutta and Volmar clearly knew of them and the way in which they were developing into prophetic visions. When she was forty-two, after Jutta's death, one of her visions commanded her to 'Say and write what you see and hear'. She said, 'Heaven was opened and a fiery light of exceeding brilliance came and permeated my whole brain, and inflamed my whole heart and my whole breast, not like a burning but like a warming flame, as the sun warms anything its rays touch'.[3] At the time of this vision, Hildegard was again ill. With the encouragement and help of Volmar and Richardis, she accepted the command to write her visions *(Scivias)* and thereby recovered. But she remained anxious about the nature of her visions, and whether the church approved. With the support of St Bernard, Abbot of Clairvaux, her writing was approved by Pope Eugenius. This gave her visions the seal of approval which was the essential foundation for her public work.

She experienced vivid scenes with colour, movement and sound, when she was awake and with her eyes open. In her books she describes these scenes in great detail, expounding on their meaning. She described them for her assistants to paint, and may have painted some herself.[4] The main body of her visions is contained in her three major books, though some were used in her letters responding to specific issues or questions put to her. The visions were always accompanied by illness, which disappeared when she had written them down.

Her descriptions of her visions and her accompanying illnesses have led modern commentators to suggest that she suffered from severe migraine attacks.[5] What she did with these visionary experiences however was not typical of migraine sufferers. Flanagan suggests that she became increasingly proficient in harnessing the experiences to her intellectual and spiritual quest into cosmological matters as well as in seeking answers to specific practical questions. She distinguished between the 'shadow of the living light' which was always present, and the 'living light' itself which she can glimpse only occasionally. In this living light she saw, knew and understood simultaneously all those things she described in her visions. Through them, and in her writings, she articulated her mission to teach and preach the Christian doctrine, and to proclaim the justice of God. In this, in many respects, she took a contemporary and orthodox approach, and her writings can be difficult for a modern reader.[6] However, the breadth of Hildegard's activities, together with the imagery in her writings and the variety of media she used to convey her experience, transcend the constraints of both religious doctrine and her own era.

'VIRIDITAS' – THE GREENING POWER

Her phenomenal output indicates her vibrant energy, in spite of her illnesses. Her textual imagery is poetic and reflects this vibrancy: 'All living creatures are sparks from the radiation of God's brilliance, and these sparks emerge from God like the rays of the sun'.[7]

Closely allied to her ideas of light and brilliance was her idea of 'viriditas' – the greening power. She powerfully uses the imagery of the lush green environment of the Rhineland, where she lived all her life, to expound her visions and her ideas. She heard the 'fiery life of the divine essence' saying, 'I awaken everything to life. The air lives by turning green and being in bloom. The waters flow as if they were alive.'[8]

This reflects the vibrancy and energy that she conveys when she is commenting on the way things are, whether in the spiritual or moral realm or in the natural and physical world. So 'the soul is the green life-force of the flesh' and 'the soul is infused throughout the human organism, just as moisture is infused throughout the Earth'.[9] She describes the soul as giving 'vitality to the marrow and veins and members of the whole body, as the tree from its root gives sap and greenness to all the branches'.[10]

Moisture and warmth nurture seeds and bring forth fruit in the natural world. Hildegard says 'the living well is the Spirit of God … the soul is a living breath of the spirit. This breath is constantly at work within us and causes us to flow, so to speak, through whatever we know, think, say or do'.[11] The Holy Spirit working in people makes them 'green and fruitful so that they bring forth noble fruits of virtue'.[12] However, if 'we give up the green vitality of these virtues and surrender to the drought of our indolence, so that we do not have the sap of life and the greening power of good deeds, then the power of our very soul will begin to fade and dry up'.[13] Depending on our willingness to accept the spirit we can also be 'sometimes green and sometimes dried-up'.[14] So being fruitful depends on moistness and the presence of the spirit, the breath of life.

Hildegard uses these images of viriditas throughout her work. In her books, her letters and her songs they succeed in creating a sense of the pulsing, connecting nature of life. What all these ideas have in common is that the life force, the vitality, connects one thing with another whether physically or morally. As Hildegard says 'everything that is in the heavens, on the earth, and under the earth, is penetrated with connectedness, is penetrated with relatedness'.[15]

THE COSMIC WHOLE

It seems clear from her writings that she was herself suffused with the sense of the world around us, the cosmos, being a unified whole. 'I am life, whole and entire ... All life has its roots in me'.[8] In her early visions she saw the universe as an egg, and in later visions as a wheel. 'The Godhead is like a wheel, a whole. In no way is it to be divided...'[16] She was very conscious of the usefulness and the limitations of analogies, and of the need not to take them literally. She uses them to good effect in stimulating in the reader the feelings she is aiming to convey, and in illuminating the variety of characteristics she herself is sensing. So the idea of the wheel which has no beginning and no end and which is a unified whole leads to the idea that God's power and work encircle and include every creature.

When everything is part of a unity, then there must be a strong connecting force. The paintings of Hildegard's visions[17] show us graphically the sense she had of the winds and the light which penetrated throughout the cosmos. She says 'the winds by their power maintain the whole universe as well as humanity in which all creation is shared ...'[18] and 'creation itself is hidden in a fire that penetrates and tests everything'.[19] She repeatedly stresses the relationships of everything to the whole, and to each other: 'every creature is linked to another, and every essence is constrained by another'.[20] These relationships have distinct patterns which are replicated throughout the cosmos. The arrangements of space are 'according to a definite standard',[21] and the human form follows the same ratios and processes. She had a strong sense of repeating patterns everywhere, an idea which modern science demonstrates in mathematical regularities, from the microcosm to the macrocosm, and in the fractal patterns underlying apparent chaos.[22]

For Hildegard, as for other thinkers of her day, humanity 'stands in the midst of the structure of the world'.[23] The rest of creation was made by God for the benefit of humanity. Yet Hildegard is clear that humanity is so much a part of nature that we cannot survive without it, and indeed that our being human depends on our relationships with the other creatures. Moreover, 'if we abuse our position to commit evil deeds, God's judgement will permit other creatures to punish us'.[24]

THE WHOLE PERSON – SOUL AND BODY

Hildegard thus had a strong sense of humanity's place as part of the whole creation, and embedded in it. She also paid a great deal of attention to the inner workings of the individual person, as a microcosm of the whole. Her approach was again holistic. The soul and the body have different roles but they are essential to each other and have to work together. They are a single reality and the living person is their working together.

This is not always a harmonious relationship. She sees the soul and body locked together in a powerful struggle, with the desires of the flesh causing the trouble. The soul has to discipline the body, subduing it, and then the soul can 'awaken in it a longing for heavenly things'.[25] Sexual activities were high on the list of the things which caused these struggles. Theologically Hildegard took the traditional approach that sexual desire other than for procreation should be repressed. In some of her writings however she showed unusual understanding of human sexuality, especially when dealing with medical and psychological problems. This arose from her understanding of the reality of the relationship between the soul, the body and the emotions.

She describes, for instance, how 'if our thoughts grow opinionated and obdurate ... the powers of virtue will be weakened and desiccated within us'.[26] These thoughts will alter our conscience, and our strength of feeling. These in turn will dry and tighten the muscular system, leaving it less responsive to the spirit. Her vision *On Human Nature* describes how the various organs of the body are connected to each other and to different emotions and illnesses. These in turn are closely connected with the qualities of the external 'winds and air'. In this way, she illustrates the interconnectedness of the internal workings of the body and the whole person together with the external environment.

There are intimate and instantaneous connections between the soul and the body, and their mutuality is absolute: 'The soul sustains the flesh, just as the flesh sustains the soul. For every deed is accomplished by the soul and the flesh'[25] and 'wherever soul and body live together in proper agreement, they attain the highest reward in mutual joy'.[27] The struggles of soul and body are an inevitable part of being human, and one potentially full of blessing. 'People work more strongly in soul and body than if they had no difficulty in doing it',[28] and 'through the distress of the body we often attain spiritual treasures'.[29] She herself had a lifetime of physical pain and suffering which led through her visions to an outpouring of creativity in her writings, music, preaching and spiritual leadership. She wrote, from personal experience, on the human struggle to use adversity positively, and demonstrated its power for creativity and transformation.

HOLISTIC EXPERIENCE

Hildegard seems to have had a deep personal awareness of the significance of engaging all our senses in our experience of life. An essential concomitant of this is getting things into balance and moderation. She was very conscious of the 'correct and balanced standard'[30] in the cosmos, and said 'the winds keep the universe in balance'.[31] She counselled moderation as 'the mother of all the virtues'.[32] She understood the connection between emotional strain and bodily weakness: 'a person who lays on herself more strain than her body can endure [will be damaged]'.[33]

There is a deep appreciation, throughout her work, of the interplay between the different parts of our selves. In commenting on the fall of Adam she says: 'he tried to know the wisdom of the Law with his intelligence, as if with his nose, but did not perfectly digest it ... in his mouth or fulfil it ... by the work of his hands'.[34] In modern terms, she saw the importance of linking our left brain thinking (analytical and logical) to our right brain thinking (imaginative, sensing and whole body). Wisdom is attainable only if all the senses are used.

To express herself, and to communicate, she used all the creative processes at her disposal. They were divine gifts: 'all the arts are derived from the breath that God sent into the human body',[35] and essential to use in living life to the full. Colours, sound, movement, poetry, drama, painting, music, singing, were all used to enhance her books, letters and public speaking. The paintings which accompany her visions for *Scivias,* reveal her interest in colours and symbolic imagery. They show how vivid were her visions, and how she was impelled to pass them on to others. They must have exercised her senses all over again in their production,[36] and contributed to her ability to articulate her visions in writing. Looking at them now, while reading her text, is a meditation in itself. The reader is drawn into the numinous world of Hildegard's own experience.

She wrote the words and music for many songs, and the nuns in her convents must have had a rich liturgical life.[37] In her own music the singing is very physical, and was for her an intimate act of the body and soul together. She experienced it like this: 'And their song goes through you so that you understand them perfectly'.[38] Modern musicians and singers still find her music powerful, and listening to her songs gives us a deep and whole experience.[39] This was intentional. In the last year of her life, writing about the role of sacred music, she said: 'the listeners might be so excited by these external things and brought into their rhythm that inwardly they might delight in their meaning'.[40]

BEING OUR OWN MYSTIC

Hildegard was an unusual woman for her day in transcending the patriarchal barriers, and she provides an important example for us. But in an era when our way of life damagingly disregards the wholeness of creation, her sense of it and her ability to convey it are even more significant for us. Her vision of creation was of an organic whole, pulsing with life, with everything appropriately connected.

At the cosmic level, she saw humanity embedded in creation and inseparable from it. Individual human beings were a microcosm of this unity. But this is a unity teeming with life in all dimensions, with all its tensions and changes, and the need to work with the grain of the dynamic life-force.

Her own life exemplified this approach. She grasped the significance of our bodily experiences as the integration of the material and the spiritual. We have to use all our senses, all aspects of ourselves, to be at one with the cosmos and ourselves. Remarkably, Hildegard has bequeathed to us a variety of gifts for us to use to do this. Her own writings, music, drama and paintings are still available to excite our senses. We can experience for ourselves her holistic approach through meditating on her paintings, reading her texts, and singing or listening to her music. In this way, she can lead us into our own mystical experience, to help us to develop our own ways of being whole, and to sense the awe and wonder of being alive and part of the whole creation.

4

Kinship with nature:
Francis of Assisi
(1181-1226)

JOHN FRANCIS GREEN

In 1181 in the town of Assisi, in the Italian Apennine mountains, a boy was born to a wealthy cloth merchant, Pietro Bernardone, and his wife Pica who came from Provence. A few kilometres north-west was the city of Perugia. The boy's name was Giovanni, but he became known as Francesco, which means the Frenchman. He grew up to be slightly under average height, with a long thin dark face, and a joyful disposition. Intuitive, intelligent, poetic, courteous and generous, he nevertheless had an iron will. He loved his mother's Provençal culture and the troubadour songs.

Italy was a series of city states, locked into economic and military rivalries. The popes were building up the secular wealth and power of the church. Pope Alexander III was in military conflict with Frederick Barbarossa, the Holy Roman Emperor, over questions of supremacy. The conflict between church and state continued under Pope Innocent III (1198-1216). Others, however, objected to the increasing wealth and power of the church, believing that followers of Christ should accept poverty, avoid property, and work among the poor. The church denounced this opposition as heretical. Francis grew up amidst this turmoil. His father had knightly ambitions for him, and Francis fought in the wars with Perugia in 1201-1202, which ended in a fiasco and personal humiliation for Francis.

An illness as a young man made Francis more thoughtful. One night a friend found him in dejection and asked, 'What is the matter, Francis, have you got married?' 'Yes,' said Francis, 'to Lady Poverty.' He travelled to Rome, and on the steps of St Peter's changed clothes with a beggar, putting on the beggar's grey hood and tunic which was to become the dress of the future Friars Minor. Travelling home, he met a leper, got off his horse, embraced him and accompanied him to the leper house, where he befriended the community. He raided his father's warehouse and sold cloth to raise money for the restoration of a small semi-derelict chapel. For this he was brought before the town council, and eventually, throwing down his clothes at his father's feet in the square, he left home to take to the road. He became known as 'il Poverello', dedicating himself to absolute poverty, preaching and teaching among the poor, the sick, and the outcasts. The high Middle Ages saw a rapid growth of towns and cities, accompanied by the increasing poverty common to such changes.

In 1210 Francis founded the Order of Friars Minor, a fraternity, not of coventual monks, but of wandering friars. This was followed by a women's order, led by his friend Clare, which we know as the Poor Clares, and a lay order known as Tertiaries. Dante Alighieri was a Franciscan Tertiary. A century earlier there had been an important reform movement against the increasing wealth and luxury of the monasteries. The Cistercian Order was founded in Brittany to revive the old Benedictine tradition and a life of subsistence on the land. But the Franciscans differed from them, rejecting the enclosed monastic life and ownership of property. The new Friars preferred the open road, and the nomadic life seen in the Gospels. This led to the rejection of money and of 'book learning', as well as priestly orders. But the two orders both saw themselves as the 'pauperes Christi', Christ's poor, devoted to asceticism, manual labour, and austere living conditions. Both saw their members as 'jongleurs' or minstrels of God, turning the world's values upside down. Both saw creation as inseparable from the Creator, and were in close contact with nature daily. Stories of 'miraculous' communication with wild creatures are common to each.

The *Canticle of the Sun*

Francis rejoiced in the beauty of creation. The earliest poem in the Italian language to have come down to us is his *Canticle of the Sun,* written in 1225-1226. It is built around a new understanding of a deep relationship with nature herself. The *Canticle* opens with an outburst of spontaneous praise:

Most High, all-powerful, good Lord, To You be praise,
glory, honour, and all blessing.
Only to You, Most High, do they belong,
and no one is worthy to call upon Your name. (vv 1, 2)[1]

Francis' fame rests on the nature stories in his life. But he was of the medieval world, and did not have the understanding of a modern ecologist. Nevertheless in 1980 he was declared the patron saint of ecology, and in 1986 the World Wide Fund For Nature called together a council of all religions at Assisi to consider the present environmental crisis.

Over the centuries there have been several important trends in Christian thought about humanity's relationship with creation. The medieval monks and nuns had a great affection for and a deep understanding of nature. But they also had a fear of demonic powers in wild places, which they had to overcome. Francis grew up surrounded by these traditions and beliefs. He was also surrounded by the folk-songs of the Italian countryside, coming from an ancient past not quite forgotten by the peasants. This folk-tradition is reflected in the Canticle:

Be praised, my Lord, for sister, our mother earth,
Who sustains and governs us,
And produces diverse fruits with coloured flowers
and grass. (v 9)

The Franciscans were very close to the common people, with daily contact with all kinds of folk, especially the peasants.

Religious communities started with groups of hermits, who settled in wild desert places to be near to God. Francis himself spent some of his time living this way. Hermits had to learn to live off the land like the animals, or they died. There are stories of them taming and befriending wild beasts. One had a wolf as a friend. Another, having lost his human companion, asked God for a replacement and was sent a bear. Maybe that tale is an example of divine humour, but they all carry the idea that humans and animals should and could co-exist. Such stories were carried by the wandering troubadours and jongleurs. Hermits and wandering friars lived in the open air surrounded by the sun, wind, and rain. We can feel Francis' sense of the open air and the elements in his *Canticle:*

> Be praised my Lord, for brother wind,
> and by air and clouds, clear skies, and all weathers,
> by which You give sustenance to Your creatures. (v 6)

Francis loved the songs and traditions of the troubadours and jongleurs. After the traumatic break with his father, he went through the mountains himself, singing praises to God in French in trouba-dour style. On this journey he was attacked by robbers, always a danger in those days for the traveller. His war experience and his break-up with his family must have made the peaceful countryside around the city, and the hermit's life, very attractive to him. He always felt the call to solitary existence. In such circumstances the sunshine must have been important to him, so like the warmth of God's love:

> May You be praised my Lord, with all Your creatures,
> especially Sir brother sun,
> through whom You lighten the day for us.
> He is beautiful and radiant with great splendour,
> he signifies You, O Most High. (vv 3, 4)

The hermits, wandering friars and remote Cistercian monks knew the value of water. The Cistercians built beside rivers, whose streams were diverted for drinking water and for drainage. The hermits sited their huts near springs or lakes. The wandering friars, often footsore and thirsty, would delight at the finding of a clear stream. Francis offers praise for sister water:

> Be praised my Lord, for sister water,
> who is very useful and humble and precious and pure. (v 7)

Francis' contacts with animals are very reminiscent of the early desert fathers. He released rabbits caught in traps. He was delighted when, on his arrival at La Verna, a flock of birds settled on him. On another occasion the greetings of birds attracted him to a particular spot in the Venetian marshes. He treated all creatures with respect, and there are countless stories in which he is involved with animals, or draws lessons from them. Bees, ants, mice were all sources for moral lessons. He clearly loved the presence of animals, and was careful not even to squash a worm. He tried to dissuade the friars from keeping pets because their endless travelling made it difficult to care for them. He also, like many of the old hermits, sometimes saw animals as demon possessed. For example there is a story in the *Legend of Perugia* about mice which he thought were so possessed. Being a medieval person, the Devil was real to him, and there are tales of his night-long struggles with demons. His world was a much more spiritually threatening place than ours. His faith kept him.

In 1213 one of the most arresting incidents of his life took place; his sermon to the birds. It was to become the story that typifies Franciscan attitudes to creation. We see Francis overcome with a great fervour, drawing upon the respect and love he had developed for nature, and showing his deep conviction in his mission. The event shows Francis' way of personifying nature which is also seen in some of the Hebrew psalms, where all of creation is called upon to praise. A near contemporary of Francis, Thomas of Celano, set down his version of the sermon in 1228:

> Among the many things he spoke to them were these words that he added: 'My brothers, birds, you should praise your creator very much and always love him; he gave you feathers to clothe you, wings so that you can fly, and whatever else was necessary for you. God made you noble among his creatures, and he gave you a home in the purity of the air; though you neither sow nor reap, he nevertheless protects and governs you without any solicitude on your part'.[2]

We probably have here a reasonably accurate account of what happened. The Franciscan preaching mission is to all of creation, not just to humankind. This reflects the early instruction attributed to Jesus to preach the gospel to all creation.[3] Having done this, Francis goes on his way rejoicing, delighted that the birds did not fly away. A miracle had taken place.

What is important in the sermon to the birds? Francis called the birds 'noble'. This shows his respect for his fellow creatures, and maybe reflects Francis as the one time candidate for knighthood. He calls them 'brothers', implying a horizontal relationship with nature which is very different from the hierarchical, vertical, relationship that the medieval world saw between nature and humankind. This sense of kinship occurs in other incidents in his life. For example, he calls the swallows his sisters. The experience of giving the sermon to the birds seems to have changed his understanding.

It is very difficult to separate the miraculous from the natural in Francis' life. Numerous incidents clearly have an element of reality, overlaid with legend. One strange story is of his having his eyes cauterised in a vain attempt to save his sight. It tells us how he talked to Brother Fire, to calm his already trembling body, reminding fire that God has created him with a splendour that all envy, and asking him to be good to him and burn him gently. The strength of Francis' own character comes out in this incident. It is a combination of miracle, reality, and Francis' own will, which makes it difficult to be sure what really happened. But the relationship with fire personified as a creature reflects what he wrote in his *Canticle:*

> Be praised my Lord, for brother fire,
> by whom the night is illumined for us,
> he is beautiful and cheerful, full of power and strong. (v 8)

Francis developed a 'courtly relationship' with creation. His early background of chivalry left a legacy of courtly behaviour. Thomas of Celano calls him a 'doughty knight for Christ'. He is also known to have called his followers 'companions of the Round Table'. The various accounts of him refer in several places to his chivalry to others and his courtesy, and these knightly qualities appear from time to time in his treatment of other creatures. He thus lived out in his mission the knightly virtues, a powerful code of behaviour and manners which may have been forgotten in the late twentieth century.

Francis was an outstanding example of the nature mystic. One way of describing nature mysticism is to say that earthly beauty captures the observer's attention, which is then directed through nature to the hidden divine beauty. Thomas of Celano shows us how Francis exercised the art of mystical contemplation:

> He embraced all things with a feeling of unheard of devotion, speaking to them of the Lord and admonishing them to praise him ... All his attention and affection he directed with his whole being to the one thing which he was asking of the Lord, not so much praying as becoming himself a prayer ... Thus, filled with a glowing fervour of spirit and his whole appearance and his soul melted, he dwelt already in the highest realms of the heavenly kingdom.[4]

Another source, the *Legend of Perugia,* says of his meeting with various creatures:

> He chatted to them with inward and outward joy, just as if they felt, understood, and could talk about God, so that many times in this way he was rapt in contemplation of God.[5]

In his *Canticle of the Sun,* we see Francis appreciating the natural creation of sun, moon, wind, flowers, fire, and even death herself. He personifies everything in a unique way. There is a joy which was very much Francis' own, which has remained characteristic of the Franciscan movement. It clearly arises from the saint's own experience of and love for nature. God is affirmed as Creator, but nature is credited with being both beautiful and valuable in her own right. The quality of his relationship with creation seems to go beyond his contemporary tradition. The whole of creation itself is made sacramental. So Francis addresses the universe as creatures kindred with himself:

> Be praised my Lord, for sister moon and the stars,
> clear and precious and lovely, they are formed in heaven.(v 5)

When Francis realised he was dying, he had himself brought to the Porziuncula, a little chapel in a wood which he and his followers had restored for their use. There he was laid on the floor, and there he died, still singing the Canticle and exhorting all creatures to praise God. He welcomed death as his sister. Legend has it that, at the moment of his death on the evening of 3 October 1226, a flock of larks, usually such day-loving birds, circled around the place where he was with loud cries. Even in death he was surrounded by the natural world.

His *Canticle* expressed an important idea. We can appreciate the goodness as well as the usefulness of creation. It was a statement about reconciliation, not just between the warring cities in Italy, but between the natural world and humanity. All creatures are brothers and sisters of each other, in our common praise of God as Creator. He has a special blessing for those who endure trials and wait for peace:

> Be praised my Lord, by all those who forgive
> for love of You and bear weakness and tribulation.
> Blessed are those who bear them in peace
> for You. Most High, they will be crowned. (vv 10, 11)

But there are a number of things in Francis' life and attitudes that we find hard to understand and appreciate in our own day. He saw the world through his own eyes in his own time. He had for example medieval ideas about personal sin:

> Woe to those who are dying in mortal sin.
> Blessed are those who are found doing Your most holy will, for
> the second death will do them no harm. (v 13)

REGAINING KINSHIP

There is something we need to recapture from Francis. We have largely lost his gift for nature mysticism. We need to recover this in the late twentieth century. We need to recapture Francis' calm and accepting attitude to the natural cycle of life and death:

> Be praised my Lord, for our sister the death of the body
> From which no one living is able to flee. (v 12)

The Franciscans have never lost his love and respect for animals and the created world. We need to learn from that. Our relationship with creation is not static. It must change and develop constantly, but in a positive way, for the good of all creatures. Until we again see all creatures as our brothers and sisters, we shall continue to destroy what we need for our own survival. Until we adopt willingly the 'priestly role of humanity' towards the rest of creation, we shall continue to fail in our appreciation of the uniqueness of St Francis of

Assisi, and so fail to learn what he tells us. This requires a final special characteristic of Francis in our own attitudes towards the earth and its creatures: humility of spirit...

> Praise and bless my Lord and give him thanks
> and serve him with great humility. (v 14)

5

The meaning and value of creation: **Thomas Aquinas** (1225–1274)

Richard Woods, O P

Like many great geniuses, Thomas of Aquino (or Thomas Aquinas, as he is usually known) died relatively young.[1] Born in the winter of 1225-1226, he died on 7 March, 1274. He was the youngest son of Lord Landulf and Lady Theodora of Aquino, who lived near Naples. At the age of five, he was sent for schooling to the Benedictines at Monte Cassino, with the confident expectation that he would someday become abbot. But as a university student in Naples in 1240, he became deeply attracted to the Order of Preachers – a new urban religious movement which combined scholarship with evangelical poverty, preaching, and a simple gospel style of life.

Thomas' family was appalled when he joined the Order and was clothed in the Dominican habit. Hoping to bring him to his senses, they kidnapped him and for over fifteen months attempted to 'deprogramme' him. Ox-like, the teenager resisted every inducement to abandon his new commitment, and was finally freed from confinement through the intervention of his mother. Sent to the Dominican house of studies at the University of Paris, Thomas soon fell under the influence of one of the most powerful minds of the age – Albert of Lauingen (c.1200-1280). In 1248, Albert took Thomas to Cologne to establish a new studium generale, a principal school for the education of young Dominicans, which eventually became the nub of a major university. There Thomas finished his initial studies, and was sent back to teach in Paris and become a master in sacred theology – the highest academic honour of the time.

Thomas' intellectual career was not an easy one. He found himself embroiled in disputes with the other masters, centering principally on the use of Aristotle by Albert, Thomas himself, and other radicals. Thomas was suspect also because of his affiliation with the Dominicans, who along with the Franciscans and members of other new religious movements living solely on alms, were resented and despised by the traditional clerical faculty and many bishops. As brilliant a debater as he was a scholar and teacher, Thomas bested some of the keenest minds in the university in formal disputation, including the future Bishop of Paris, Stephen Tempier, and future Archbishop of Canterbury, John Pecham. After Thomas' premature death, both took pains to ensure that his teaching was condemned at the universities of Paris and Oxford.

Although immersed in controversy most of his life as a professor, Thomas had important friends and allies, including King Louis IX of France and Pope Urban IV, at whose request he composed the liturgical texts for the feast of Corpus Christi – perhaps the most elegantly poetic and deeply religious of all Thomas' works. Justly famed for his huge handbooks, the unfinished *Summa Theologiae* and the *Summa Contra Gentes,* as well as his philosophical commentaries and theological treatises, Thomas would have understood himself primarily as a scripture scholar. His commentaries on the gospels, especially the Gospel of John, include his finest contributions to spirituality as well as to biblical studies.

In 1274, Thomas was summoned to the Ecumenical Council at Lyon, at which, it was hoped, Eastern and Western Christendom would be reunited. That was not to be. Nor would Thomas be there. The previous December, on the feast of St Nicholas, he seems to have suffered an accident of some kind, most likely a cerebral haemorrhage, which left him partially impaired in speech and unable to write. En route to the Council, he suffered further injury when he struck his head against an overhanging branch. Taken to the Cistercian abbey of Fossanuova, he died there in the company of his fellow friars, both Franciscan and Dominican, as well as the monks and several relatives.

Within three years, Thomas' old opponent, Tempier, and Edward Kilwardby, the Dominican Archbishop of Canterbury, succeeded in having over one hundred propositions from his works condemned as heretical because of their Aristotelian flavour. At Oxford, the condemnation was repeated in 1284 by Kilwardby's successor, John Pecham. Thomas' supporters resisted strenuously. In 1309, the Dominican Order declared Thomas' teaching to be the official doctrine of the Order. By 1315, complete copies of his writings were ordered to be made available in all houses of study and major priories. Two years later, materials were gathered to support his canonisation, and on 14 July, 1323 Pope John XXII formally enrolled Thomas among the saints. In 1325 the Bishop of Paris revoked the condemnation of 1277, although Thomas was never formally rehabilitated at Oxford. In 1567, however, he was declared a Doctor of the Church. Closer to our own times, in 1880 Pope Leo XIII recognised Thomas as the patron of all Catholic universities.

Poet, preacher, and philosopher, Thomas belongs to humanity, not merely to Catholicism or even Christianity. Generations of thinkers in many traditions have come to find in him a valued exponent of the 'middle way' between methodological scepticism and uncritical fundamentalism, as well as between materialism and idealism. Not without reason, Thomas' cosmological speculations, particularly his vision of the universe as an organic, interrelated whole mediating the beauty, majesty, and delight of God to human and other creatures, are finding a new and sympathetic audience today among both scientists and seers.

THE MEANING AND VALUE OF CREATION

While Thomas' doctrine of creation is indebted to Albert the Great, it possesses distinctively original characteristics, particularly in regard to cosmological theory. Because of its Aristotelian tone, it differs pointedly from the aesthetic, Platonic theories that preceded it in the long dialogue among philosophers and theologians. Leo Elders writes that:

> In the great medieval Summae, in particular in St Thomas' works, the treatise of creation is the crowning piece of metaphysics. Instead of monism or dualism an entirely new doctrine of God and creation is developed. A loving decision by a spiritual being to make the world replaces the natural process of emanation. The study of creation also leads us to a new understanding of created beings.[2]

From beginning to end, Thomas' doctrine is theological. God remains the central focus of his inquiry, which is intent on showing that the universe is wholly the product of God's creative design and intent, is maintained at every moment of its existence by God's power, and wholly reflects God's goodness and love. From our perspective, in turn, the created universe as a whole and in all its variety, multiplicity, and complexity mediates God's presence, wisdom and goodness. It is sacramental.

This was radical enough to earn Thomas unremitting opposition, especially because of his insistence that science and philosophy could not definitely prove that the universe had a beginning in time – a problem that still perplexes scientific cosmology. For Thomas, the sole warrant for his insistence was faith in the revealed word of God in scripture. For him 'creation' does not simply mean producing something original. It refers to the fact that there is anything at all:

> Creation implies a thing's existence in fact, not that it has been achieved as the result of a preceding process. No approach to being is involved, nor any transmutation. What is stated is just initial reality coupled with a reference to the creator. In this sense, creation is original freshness related to God.[3]

Thus for Thomas the term 'creation' designated 'the emanation … of the whole of being from the universal cause,'[4] the totality of being in all its expanse, unity and multiplicity, precisely as each creature and all creatures together are immediately related to God as their origin and the equally immediate cause of their present existence. For Thomas, the universe is a unique, organically interrelated whole immediately and directly dependent on God for its existence.

The underlying question Thomas faced has been raised again in our time by Martin Heidegger: Why does anything exist rather than nothing at all? Not just in terms of being-in-general, but of particular, existing beings – all of them and the whole. Ultimately, this is the fundamental question of metaphysics and, indeed, of all philosophy.[5] The meaning, value, and purpose of the physical universe itself, including ourselves and all other creatures, is at stake. It is a matter not only of speculative interest and attitude, but also of activity, in particular with regard to the exploitation and destruction of the natural world.

Thomas' view of the universe has important implications for contemporary cosmology and environmental concerns. First of all, unlike many theologians and scientists right up to the present time, Thomas was acutely conscious that its primary and essential character is reflected in the word 'universe' itself: the universe is one, a unified whole. And whether finite or infinite in extent and duration, it is a unity precisely because its very being depends solely on the One God. In effect, its unity depends upon its createdness.[6] This leads to the second of Thomas' major tenets: God is the only and immediate cause of the existence of the universe. Precisely because the existence of the universe as a whole and in all of its constituent elements is what 'creation' actually refers to, God and God alone can be the original source. God didn't make the universe 'out of' anything, nor did God need any assistance. And if the word 'God' has any meaning at all in this regard, it refers to the infinite power and presence that alone can account for the existence of everything.

But if God alone is the original cause of the being of anything and everything, so too only God can maintain and preserve in existence the universe and everything in it. Although the constituent elements of creation may alter in time and space, the identity of the universe as a whole and the continued existence of every quantum of mass-energy in whatever form bespeaks a power beyond the universe which supports the process of change itself. Creation for Thomas is thus a continuing action.[7]

CREATION CONTROVERSIES

Two complex issues greatly vexed Thomas' contemporaries at the University of Paris and occasioned some heated intellectual battles with them. These concerned the eternity of the world versus its beginning in time, and the problem of universal causality versus particular causes, especially the problem of multiplicity of form.

Abstruse as these may sound to us today, both matters touch on contemporary issues in physics being debated by Stephen Hawking and other physicists: Did the universe have a beginning in time? Is there only one universe or a multitude, perhaps even an infinity of universes 'parallel' to this one? How is it that the universe is coherent? That everything seems to interrelate? That our mathematics, odd as they might be, actually pertain to the observable universe? How is it that chemical elements, physical processes, and the underlying relationships of matter and energy, the speed of light, and so forth, seem to pertain wherever we look in the universe? Because of his penetrating study of Aristotelian philosophy and especially the scientific implications of the new cosmology being reintroduced into Europe from Aristotle's Arab commentators, Thomas opted for the least popular position in each case.

Against Augustine of Hippo and the whole Christian Platonic tradition, Thomas taught that 'time itself is contained in the universe, and therefore when we speak about creation we should not inquire at what time it happened'.[8] Further, 'creation precisely states a principle of origin, but not necessarily a principle of duration'.[9] The world could have existed eternally, as Aristotle held, even without compromising its total dependence on God: 'God is before the world in duration, yet before does not mean a priority of time, but of eternity, or perhaps, if you like, an endlessness of imaginary time'.[10] But 'that the world must have existed always is not a necessary truth, nor can it be demonstratively proved'.[11] Thomas maintained that given the limits of science and philosophy (their absolute limits, not just the limitations of the day), the question could not be answered one way or the other. Only God's revealed word could give such assurance. The beginning of the world in time remained for him an item of faith, not of reason.

It was his daring views on these subjects, which were diametrically opposed to those of St Bonaventure and Alexander of Hales, among others, which singled Thomas out for attack. On the other hand, the philosophical faculty at Paris seemed to have welcomed and appreciated Thomas' honesty and courage, noticeably among them Siger of Brabant,[12] whose doctrines were also condemned in 1277. Thomas also had many supporters in England.

GOD'S EXTRAVAGANZA

Thomas insisted that the multiplicity and richness of creation was as much a reflection of God's nature as was the unity of the world:

> For [God] brought forth into being in order that His goodness might be communicated to creatures, and be represented by them; and because his goodness could not be adequately represented by one creature alone, he produced many and diverse creatures, [so] that what was wanting to one in the representation of the divine goodness might be supplied by another. For goodness, which in God is simple and uniform, in creatures is manifold and divided: and hence the whole universe together participates the divine goodness more perfectly, and represents it better than any single creature whatever.[13]

Thomas' universe is not a monolithic block: for him, as for Gerard Manley Hopkins, multiplicity, variety, and even inequality mirror the infinite goodness and wild vitality of God within the unity of creation – an idea contained today in the growing importance of ecological diversity. Evil itself is only permitted to mar the perfection of elements within creation because overcoming such defects contributes further to the perfection of the whole.

> It is the part of the best agent to produce an effect which is best in its entirety; but this does not mean that God makes every part of the whole the best absolutely, but in proportion to the whole; in the case of an animal, for instance, its goodness would be taken away if every part of it had the dignity of an eye. Thus, therefore, God also made the universe to be best as a whole, according to the mode of a creature; whereas He did not make each single creature best, but one better than another.[14]

Even so, for Thomas the wholeness and unity of creation remains its primary characteristic and most perfectly radiates God's own goodness, unity, and love. The universe in its entirety is not only the masterpiece of the divine artist, but the first of the sacraments.

THOMAS, ALBERT AND ECKHART

Philosophically and theologically, the doctrine of creation is not a matter of straightforward deduction. From a historical perspective, Thomas was certainly right that philosophers and theologians differed greatly as to what could and could not be established about creation from human reasoning alone.

His own concerns were always more metaphysical than scientific, nor do we find the rhapsodic delight in creation that appears, for instance, in Francis of Assisi or the Celtic tradition. Thomas more greatly resembles Meister Eckhart, for whom creation in general, and in particular instances, is more a matter for thoughtful reflection on the wisdom, power, and love of God than an occasion for experiencing God. He admitted that possibility with typical reservation. Temperamentally Thomas and Eckhart preferred to *think* their way to God. They differed strikingly from their common mentor, Albert, who was fascinated by the details of what things are, whereas Thomas was interested only in books and people.[15]

WINDS OF CHANGE: PORTENTS OF THE RENAISSANCE

Thomas' approach presaged the scientific reappraisal of the natural world in the exciting years of the Italian Renaissance, but paradoxically the enthusiastic humanism of that period led to an eventual demotion of creation to the status of a cosmic machine. In her important book *The Death of Nature,* Carolyn Merchant describes the transition in chilling terms:

> The removal of animistic, organic assumptions about the cosmos constituted the death of nature – the most far-reaching effect of the Scientific Revolution. Because Nature was now viewed as a system of dead, inert particles moved by external, rather than inherent forces, the mechanical framework itself could legitimate the manipulation of nature. Moreover, as a conceptual frame-

work, the mechanical order had associated with it a framework of values based on power, fully compatible with the directions taken by commercial capitalism."[16]

The holistic, organic and spiritual element so prominent in Thomas' views evaporated under the dry eye of Baconian and Newtonian science. Edward Conze comments: 'As a result of Newton's intellectual labours a dark shadow has been cast over the spiritual radiance of the universe, and the celestial harmonies have become nearly inaudible ever since'.[17]

There are ethical and aesthetic principles implicit in Thomas' teaching on creation which are relevant today. Not least of these is the holiness of creation as an effective sign of God's presence, power and love. Because creation is a creative manifestation of God, 'to hold creatures cheap is to slight divine power',[18] or in stronger language, 'to curse irrational things as creatures of God is blasphemous, to curse them for themselves is valueless and vain'.[19] To abuse creatures is an affront to the creator, a rejection of blessing and love. Environmental exploitation is actually sinful. Official church teaching is only beginning to recognise this, although one to two hundred species are lost every twenty-four hours.

HUMANITY'S PLACE IN CREATION

Thomas' sacramental approach to the universe offers hope for seeing creation as worthy of the reverence and care due to the holy. His understanding of the universe's 'original freshness related to God', so daringly radical and condemned in his own time, became a major resource for Meister Eckhart and other mystics and theologians who followed. But do we also detect an anthropocentric bias – that all creation is a gift of God for as well as to the human race? Are we not only the caretakers but the inheritors of Eden?

Thomas' answer is undoubtedly yes. But that does not license us to do whatever we wish with nature. Our ethical responsibility in the face of the overwhelming generosity of God revealed in creation impels us to respect nature for what it is, not for what we can make it.[20] His approach to and understanding of the universe as a unified, holistic interface through which God is revealed to the mind and the heart, is increasingly recognised as a resource in the developing dialogue among physicists, theologians and spiritual seekers. Thus for Thomas, as for an increasing number of astronomers and physicists, to explore the universe humbly and reverently is not only to seek the mind of God, but to learn again to recognise the signs of divine presence, power, and love.

6

Recovering wisdom:
Meister Eckhart
(c.1260-1327)

John Doyle

Johannes Eckhart, born about 1260 in Hockheim, near Erfurt on the northern edge of Thuringia, entered the Dominicans as a young man. He held various administrative and academic posts in the Dominican provinces of Teutonia and Saxony, interspersed with periods in the University of Paris where he received the title of Meister, and twice held a chair in theology previously occupied by Thomas Aquinas. He was in regular contact with the Beguines, a spiritual movement of lay women which existed on the fringes of religious life. He influenced and was influenced by them, especially at Strasbourg, which was a great centre of mysticism and home to many communities of the Beguines.

Not much is known about Eckhart's personal life. His ideas come to us mostly through the detailed notes of his sermons recorded by the nuns to whom he ministered. These sermons were preached in the vernacular, a practice frowned on by many, but which resulted in Eckhart having a significant influence on the development of the German language. It is in the realm of language that Eckhart's mystical pedigree shines through, rather than in particular mystical experiences which dominated much of the spiritual writings of this period. Eckhart's presentation of the spiritual journey in concepts which are paradoxical, mercurial and yet deeply incisive brought him before the Inquisition.

Eckhart lived amongst great social and political turmoil. The Middle Ages were coming to an end. Political and religious institutions of the day were not meeting the needs of the people. In this situation various spiritual movements arose, seeking a radical spirituality in the face of the complacency in the church. These movements had their own inconsistencies and extremes, so an atmosphere was created in which any innovative expressions of spiritual truths were treated with suspicion and hostility. Eckhart's dealings with the Beguines, many of whom sought spiritual direction from the Dominicans, was a significant factor in the later condemnation of his ideas. The Beguines themselves became a suspect minority in the church.

ECKHART'S SPIRITUALITY

Eckhart does not dwell on the nuts and bolts of the Christian tradition. He takes the basic doctrine as read. In his preaching he leads the listener into the heart of the spiritual journey, into those aspects which are beyond doctrine and which can unite people of different religious traditions. Ecumenism, however, was not Eckhart's concern. At the core of Eckhart's spiritual teaching rests his passionate belief in the spark of the divine, which resides in the depths of the soul, and which plays a vital role in allowing for the possibility of our return to the Godhead from which we have emerged. The presence of a divine element within the human has always been part of Christian tradition, but has been overshadowed by our concern with the fallen nature of humanity. For Eckhart, however, the spiritual life hinges on the spark of the divine residing in the depths of each person.

For Eckhart, all life emanates from its source within the Godhead. In describing the act of creation, Eckhart employs the metaphor of 'boiling' (*bullitio* or *ebullitio*), first used by Plotinus the Christian Platonist. The Godhead 'springs up' or 'bubbles up' and 'boils over' in an unparalleled act of love and compassion. Creation flows out of this superabundant source. In that moment we experience ourselves as being separated. We enter a new relationship with God of whom we were once a part. When we flow out of the Godhead, God in some sense comes into being with our creation, because it is only in the experience of apparent separation that we cry out, 'God'.

> God becomes when all creatures say 'God' – then God comes to be. When I subsisted ... in the river and font of Godhead, no one asked me where I was going or what I was doing: there was no one to ask me. When I flowed forth, all creatures said 'God'. If anyone asked me, 'Brother Eckhart, when did you leave your house?' Then I must have been in there.[1]

This flowing out from the Godhead provides the context of our spiritual journey. The desire of the soul is to return to the Godhead, to that place where 'God unbecomes'. True to the mystical tradition Eckhart leads us into a world where logical, reasoned arguments become redundant, where we encounter the mystery of the divine which lies beyond linear rational thinking. Eckhart makes full use of the paradoxical nature of the divine. He presents the 'is–ness' of God often in terms of the nothingness of creatures:

> ... In God there is light and being, and in creatures there is darkness and nothingness, since what is in God is light and being, in creatures is darkness and nothing-ness.[2]

As we ponder the being of God and the nothingness of creatures we come across another sermon in which Eckhart claims that:

> God is not being or goodness. Goodness adheres to being and does not go beyond it: for if there were not being there would be no goodness, and being is even purer than goodness. God is not 'good', or 'better' or 'best'. Whoever should say God is good would do Him ... injustice ...[3]

God is beyond the power of language to describe. If we think we have found a description, in the end we have to admit God is not that. God cannot be 'this' or 'that', cannot be contained in time or space, because God is unseparated from all things, yet is within everything. So we arrive at the paradox of the 'nothingness of God', and also the 'nothingness' of creatures because their meaning is found only in God. Eckhart finds God most importantly in our inmost soul, and also in every created thing, animate or inanimate:

God is closer to me than I am to myself: my being depends on God's being near me and present to me. So He is also in a stone or a log of wood,only they do not know.[4]

THE GOD WITHIN

After concluding that God is essentially different from creatures, Eckhart begins to expand on the way in which God is intimately connected with creatures. Their existence from one moment to the next is dependent on God's presence. The key to this connection is the 'summit' or 'spark' of the soul. This is clouded in mystery as Eckhart has to avoid placing the soul on a par with God. Yet clearly this 'spark' is the spark of the divine present in us. Because of this idea Eckhart was accused of pantheism, which is nature worship. But he was expounding the notion of God within nature ('panentheism'), where creation, rather than being equal to God, is in fact a place where the divine is intimately present. In this he followed the same tradition as Thomas Aquinas, who died when Eckhart was fourteen.

But Eckhart must also guard against presenting the spark of the soul as simply being another 'thing' among things, just another object. It is an aspect of the soul that is united with God:

... As I have said before, there is something in the soul that is so near akin to God that it is one and not united ...[5]

Sometimes Eckhart relates this 'summit of the soul' to the mind or the intellect. Here he shows his Dominican bias which sees the intellect as the highest manifestation of the divine in humans. There was much conflict on this issue between the Dominicans and the Franciscans who valued love in action rather than scholarship, and it became another factor which influenced the condemnation of some of Eckhart's ideas.

The spark of intellect ... is none other than a tiny spark of the divine nature, a divine light ...[6].

This notion of the spark of the soul, while pivotal, is nonetheless fluid and difficult to pin down. It is the birth of 'the Word' in the soul, which provides us with the possibility of return to the Godhead.

THE BIRTH OF THE WORD

Having accepted the presence of the spark of the divine in the human, what then are the means by which the birth of 'the Word' takes place in the soul? For Eckhart a key attitude is that of 'awareness' or 'attention'. We can take for granted the presence of the divine within us, but our task is to grow in our awareness of this presence.

> ... So man is more blessed than a stone or a piece of wood
> because he is aware of God and knows how close God is to him.
> And I am the more blessed, the more I realise this.[7]

This awareness is connected with knowledge and understanding. As we grow in our openness to the divine presence within, so too our knowledge of the divine deepens. This is not knowledge about God, but rather knowledge which enables us to penetrate the very heart of the divine. The possibility of exploring the heart of divinity, which is our task, is itself dependent on God's grace.

One aspect of Eckhart's teaching distinguishing him from the mysticism in vogue at the time is his emphasis on everyday life as the place where we encounter the divine. If we seek more of God through special meditations or devotions, and fail to find him in the everyday things of life, we will be disappointed. Indeed the concentration on our special devotions may actually prevent us from finding God. '... Whoever seeks God in a special way gets the way and misses God ...'[8] Here are echoes of the East: 'Before enlightenment chop wood and carry water, after enlightenment chop wood and carry water'. This contrasts sharply with the preoccupation with visions, ecstasies and stigmata prevalent amongst some of the Beguines and other spiritual movements of the time. Eckhart valued the emphasis on voluntary poverty espoused by these groups, but was very aware of how any spiritual practice can become a distraction on the journey. In his *Counsels on Discernment* he speaks of penitence as:

> A complete lifting up of the mind away from all things into God
> ... and if you are impeded in this by any exterior works,
> whether it be fasting, keeping vigil, reading or whatever else,
> give it up ... because God has no regard for what your works
> are, but for what your devotion and intention in the works are.[9]

ON BEING AND DOING

Eckhart's emphasis is on being over doing. If we are authentic in our being our actions will be coloured by this. This focus on being is further emphasised in the two over-arching attitudes which open the person to the birth of God as the Word in the soul, which in turn begins the return of the soul to its source in the Godhead, whence it came. 'Active or radical detachment' and 'letting-go', at all levels, are the way to the birth of the Word in the soul.

> ... If you would find this noble birth, you must leave the crowd
> and return to the source and ground whence you came. All the
> powers of the soul, and all their works – these are the crowd.
> Memory, understanding and will, they will diversify you, and
> therefore you must leave them all, sense perceptions, imagina-
> tion, or whatever it may be that in which you seek to find
> yourself.[10]

This form of radical detachment is complemented by the more passive attitude of letting-go. Both of these qualities offer the possibility of avoiding the seduction of the illusions of this world:

> For truly, so long as created things console you and can console
> you, never will you find true consolation. But ... when nothing
> but God can console you, then truly God does console you, and
> with him everything that is joy consoles you.[11]

What, then, is Eckhart's view of the natural world? Is it a distraction from our true journey? Eckhart is however showing us that we can relate to the natural world as a mirror, where our own ego-concerns are simply reflected back to us. An example of this is where we see nature as something to be exploited for financial gain. We may even project our image of God onto the natural world, so that it is reflected back in confirmation of our particular perception of the divine. For Eckhart, radical detachment and letting-go allows the created world to become a window into the divine, a window into a reality outside our control, a window into deep mystery. In the birth of the Word in the soul there is no-thing, all things reveal their transparency and thus their true nature as windows into the divine.

TRANSFORMATION

When we are ready and open to God's grace the birth of the
Word within us takes place in a spontaneous way, and indeed
Eckhart says once we are empty God cannot contain this outflow of
grace:

> You should know, God cannot leave anything void or unfilled,
> God and nature cannot endure that anything should be empty
> or void. And so, even if you think you can't feel Him and are
> wholly empty of Him, that is not the case.[12]

For Eckhart this birth of the Word in the soul is entwined with the
birth of the Word as Logos, and the birth of Jesus as the Word in
time. Also, in the same way as he gives priority to being over doing,
so too the effect of the birth of the Word in the soul is not primarily
to be sought in external manifestations, but rather in an inner transformation which may well be subtle in terms of what can be noticed
from the outside. We know that the birth has fully taken place,
according to Eckhart, when:

> you have reached the point where nothing is grievous or hard to
> you, and where pain is not pain to you, when everything is
> perfect joy to you, then your child has really been born.[13]

In case we might despair in the face of this seemingly impossible task
Eckhart states elsewhere:

> You may think that as long as words can move you to joy or
> sorrow you are imperfect. That is not so. Christ was not so …
> No saint ever lived or ever will attain to the state where pain
> cannot hurt him nor pleasure please.[14]

The moment when the birth of the Word takes place is for
Eckhart a moment of breakthrough; the outflow from the source has
come to its outer limits and now the return begins. The return to the
unity of the Godhead happens when we let go of multiplicity, to
experience the inner unity of the still centre point of the spark of the
soul. A second birth has taken place, and the soul is again in that
place where 'God unbecomes'. In this context Eckhart said: 'I pray
God to rid me of God', which is a prayer for the return to unity
where there is no one to call upon God. All shall be one. The return

hinges on our identifying with the Son. It is the mystery of the incarnation where the divine becomes intimately involved with the human. For Eckhart this is possible because all of creation is continuously rebirthed in the incarnation:

> The Father begets His Son unceasingly, and furthermore I say,
> he begets me as His Son and the same Son. I say even more: not
> only does He beget me as His Son, but He begets me as Himself
> and Himself as me, and me as His being and His nature ... All
> that God works is one: therefore he begets me as His Son
> without any difference.[15]

This may seem deepest heresy, but Eckhart is viewing things from God's perspective, dominated by unity of being and unity of act. Everything in our experience of history unfolding is part of the initial 'boiling over' of love within the Godhead. But we must be willing to let go into the divine essence of both Father and Son. Then we are transformed. But Eckhart reminds us not to get lost in the experience. We must leave our ecstacy if faced with human need:

> ... Even if a man were in a rapture ... and knew a sick man who
> needed some soup from him, I should think it far better you left
> the rapture for love and would serve the needy man in greater
> love.[16]

The doing here flows naturally from the being. A person in the transformed state may show no outward signs nor observe any rituals. They do not require them:

> ... Such people are very hard to recognise. When others fast,
> they eat, when others watch, they sleep, when others pray, they
> are silent ... They need absolutely nothing, for they are in
> possession of the city of their true birthright.[17]

The crowning of the spiritual journey is the return to the Godhead. Traditionally spoken of in terms of the Beatific Vision, Eckhart expresses this experience in terms of our return to the source, to the river, to the fount of the Godhead.

> When I return to God ... none will ask me whence I came or
> where I have been. No one missed me, for there God unbe-
> comes.[18]

DETACHMENT – LETTING GO

Central to Eckhart's teaching are the key attitudes of 'radical detachment' and 'letting go'. We live in a world crazed by addictive behaviours, whether drugs, drink, sex, food, work, relationships, television, shopping, power. Eckhart's way may help us to return to a place where we know again our own basic goodness, the spark of the divine, becoming aware of our participation in divinity.

His teaching contradicts sharply the advertising slogans which vie for our attention every moment. Our senses are under constant bombardment and we easily become victim to the vast seductive power of consumerism. Perhaps consumerism itself is simply a manifestation of our spiritual malaise. Like Eckhart we too encounter many groups peddling their own spiritual wares, offering us the keys to the kingdom, the three steps to heaven. Clearly these groups are emerging because a very real vacuum is there to be filled. As old structures crumble and fall there is always a time of transition before the new structures emerge. If that were not so we would be in danger of pouring new wine into old wineskins. But there is great danger in this time because of our natural need for stability, our need for security, our need to believe that somebody is steering the ship and knows where it is going and how it is going to get there.

Eckhart is so refreshing because in facing a similar time of turmoil he does not look for security in external structures. Neither does he allow us to put up camp for long on any part of the spiritual journey: if our desire is the lushness of the green pastures of ecstasy and visions, he calls us on; if we wish to rest in the security of structured prayers and devotions, he calls us on; if we glory in the desert of pain and suffering, he calls us on. Our souls can contain the whole universe and so it is not appropriate to linger too long on any one part of the great journey of the soul. He calls us to rediscover the pulse of the divine beating consistently, though almost imperceptibly, within, the only basis for authentic connection with the outer world of people and things, and of course 'no-things'.

7

The soul's journey –
The Divine Comedy:
Dante Alighieri
(1265-1321)

JEAN HARDY

Before Dante's birth, Italy, and Florence, were violently divided by the two factions of the Guelfs and the Ghibellines. The Guelfs, the group into which Dante was born, were the citizens and merchants who wanted civic liberty for Florence, and who looked to the Pope for support in their cause. The Ghibellines were more aristocratic and upheld the Holy Roman Emperor. These groups were flexible and everchanging; in fact, Dante's eventual fate was related to a split within the Guelf party, which was in power in Florence for most of his life. Dante expected to take an active part in the politics of his time; his vision of political and social life was intrinsically linked with his view of community and its relationship to the spiritual path of the individual. It was a violent, warring and passionate period, with splits between Church and City State, full of the experience of enmity and horror.

Thus Dante was from the beginning of his adult life involved in politics. In his own life he faced the grimmest realities; *The Divine Comedy* was written during long years of exile from Florence. Indeed, an understanding of his hard experience is necessary in order to grasp the significance of his great inspired work, which is the search through pain and terror for an overarching harmony and the deep power of love.

DANTE'S LIFE

Dante Alighieri, a native of Florence, was born in 1265 to a well-to-do family. His mother died when he was about five, his father when he was twelve. He was then brought up by his stepmother. He was well educated, learning Latin and also the language and literature of Provence. He studied philosophy, poetry, science and theology and read constantly. He was particularly influenced by the writing of Thomas Aquinas. He was of course a poet and a writer himself, and mixed freely with artists and musicians.

The best-known story about Dante is his first glimpse of Beatrice. He met her first when he was eight – Beatrice was a year younger – and then occasionally later in his teens and early twenties. Their formal acquaintance was slight; she married someone else, and died in 1290 in her early twenties. But the sight of Beatrice awoke in Dante the knowledge of love, the glimpse of eternity.

In 1302 Dante was exiled from Florence on pain of death by burning. From then until his death in 1321 at the age of 56, he wandered around Italy and Europe, sometimes joined by his children (he had married in about 1296). He supported the Holy Roman Emperor Henry VII until Henry's death in 1313, for he looked in the latter part of his life towards a world power which would unite the whole world in peace and community. He became effectively a Ghibelline, often being known at this period as 'the Ghibelline'. He began publishing *The Divine Comedy* in 1314 and finished it well before his death.

THE DIVINE COMEDY: JOURNEY OF THE SOUL: SOME INTERPRETATIONS

Dante accepted that there are many layers of meaning within his work – the literal, the allegorical, the moral and the spiritual.[1] Dorothy Sayers, in her introduction to her translation of the *Comedy,* speaks of the work as a great allegory of the soul's journey, as relevant now as when it was written. It treats the person in the Christian and Catholic traditions as a spiritual and rational being. Hell, 'the grim substructure, is only there for the sake of the city whose walls and spires stand up and take the morning; it is for the vision of God in the *Paradiso* that all the rest of the allegory exists'.[2] All the terror is contained within the far larger vision of Love.

The Florentine psychiatrist Roberto Assagioli (1888–1974) used the *Divine Comedy* as a basis for developing psychosynthesis, a transpersonal psychotherapy. Within psychosynthesis there is a theory of human nature and healing very different from the kinds of understanding that we have in our present culture. This approach is explored in *A Psychology with a Soul*,[3] and provides a basis for this chapter.

A Jungian writer, Helen Luke, in her book *Dark Wood to White Rose: a study of meanings in Dante's Divine Comedy*,[4] interprets the *Comedy* in a way most helpful to our modern understanding. She sees the journey as the change from unconscious and unaware living, from living driven by the unknown forces that block us from the source of all being – the 'sins' in medieval terms – to conscious awareness. It is in such consciousness that we can bear at last to see the true reality of things, which is paradise.

THE DIVINE COMEDY

The experience of the poem was placed in the year 1300, at Easter, a year when Dante was midway through his own life. It is a journey through hell and purgatory, into paradise.

The journey through hell

Midway this way of life we're bound upon,
I woke to find myself in a dark wood,
Where the right road was wholly lost and gone.
Ah me! how hard to speak of it – that rude
And rough and stubborn forest! The mere breath
Of memory stirs the old fear in the blood;
It is so bitter, it goes nigh to death.

Thus Dante begins this story in the dark wood. From that wood, he can see a mountain some way off, lighted by the sun. At the top of this mountain is another wood on the edge of paradise. However, a leopard, a lion and a she-wolf, the sins of pride, lust and envy, bar his direct way. The only alternative path is the way down, through hell. Dante realises that the way to paradise must be through knowing and experiencing hell, and he concedes to this necessity.

Dante at this point meets Virgil, the Roman poet he greatly respects, who represents reason and the mind. Virgil has been sent by Beatrice to guide Dante. Setting off on their journey, down and down go Dante and Virgil, through the nine circles of the sins of hell, meeting and talking with people in various torments of fire and ice, plagued by demons, covered in filth, with heads twisted backwards and limbs distorted, with hideous diseases. Eventually they reach the Satan, 'the ill Worm that pierces the World's core', 'toward which all weight bears down from everywhere'.[5] They have to clamber over him, over his hideous shank and genitals, the very base of hell. They have come to terms with the deepest ills within themselves.

And then they find themselves climbing upwards at last, through a new birth, out of a round hole, and emerge from hell. They have been in a place where there is no sense of the beauty of the natural world, and they come out 'to look once more upon the stars'.[6]

Hell: facing the void

The experience of hell is something which we all reach at least once in our lives: the point at which the values and the structures that have supported us since childhood, which have been given us by family and society, and by which we have unconsciously lived, no longer hold. Helen Luke puts it thus: it is 'the moment when we awaken to know that we are lost – to realise, as Jung says, that the ego is not master in the house, that we are stumbling around in the dark, and that our complacent goals of power, success, respectability, rebellion, uplift, or a thousand others are empty and meaningless'.[7] The void stares us in the face.

From this dark place Dante saw the fair wood on the edge of paradise, where the human race could be, were it not for all the 'unconscious material' in Jungian terms, the 'sin' in medieval terms, which we have to face and work through. This is the human lot, which none of us can escape though many attempt to do so by opting out in a whole variety of ways. Hell is where we suffer without knowing why. Purgatory, the place that Dante and Virgil reached at the end of this first stage, is where we still suffer, but gladly, knowing we are within reach of finding our true selves, and experiencing the possibility of paradise.

Love, in the form of Beatrice, sends us reason and human wisdom, in the shape of Virgil, to assist us if we will accept it but reason can only assist us to the edge of paradise. Beyond that it is all love and divine knowledge, which help us begin to face the awesomeness of the reality of the universe. But at the beginning we cannot bear very much reality.

There is no other way to search for wisdom and wholeness than by facing the void. This means looking at the evil of which you are potentially capable, and you cannot refuse the awareness of suffering. But hell is essentially about living unconsciously: it echoes Jesus' words, 'They know not what they do'. This driven unconsciousness and lack of awareness is the source of all evil. Hell is collective as well as personal – societies as well as people who live without spiritual truth. We are driven by the forces we will not face. We project these forces onto others, make 'us' and 'them', 'good' and 'bad', and attempt to destroy the badness in ourselves by projecting it onto others and then trying to destroy or defeat them in the outside world around us.

In the *Comedy*, hell is arranged in nine circles, each representing a particular sin. These sins are the things we have to know, acknowledge and work through in ourselves during our lifetime experiences. But even before Dante and Virgil entered the gates of hell, they met the people who had refused the journey at all: those who had chosen not to truly live and who would not search for their true nature and potential. They refused self-knowledge from the beginning.

The journey through purgatory

The climate and geography of purgatory is very different from that of hell. Hell is terrible, stinking and underground. But from purgatory you are in sight of the heavens and the stars. 'The great Mountain of Purgatory rises in a pure sunlit solitude out of the windswept southern sea'.[8] It is so high that when you emerge from

hell you cannot see the top of it. Dante and Virgil come into this
scene just before daybreak. They see an angel, the first of many and
a sure sign of the presence of God. The angel came with a ship full
of souls eager, as a community rather than as separated individuals, to
climb Mount Purgatory, to:

> slough away the filth
> That will not let you see God's countenance.[9]

Before they come to the edge of purgatory they meet souls who
are having to wait to enter. These are those guilty in medieval terms
of being excommunicated, dying without repentance. The highest
group of these waiting are 'the preoccupied' – those so busy with the
world's affairs that they have no time to consider their own souls.

Dante is carried up in his sleep by St Lucy to the bottom of three
differently coloured stairs leading to St Peter's Gate. They are
accepted by God's Angel through the great gate into purgatory; they
enter hearing music, the music of the spheres, which like the angels
is now always around. Dante and Virgil next traverse the seven
circles of purgatory, all full of people representing the ways in which
love can be misused. They have to travel at one point through a
great pall of smoke, and at another need to brave a huge wall of fire.

As Dante and Virgil reach the top of the seventh circle, they at last
come to the sacred wood on the edge of paradise that Dante had
seen so longingly at the beginning, from the dark wood. Here Virgil,
reason, can take him no further and bids him farewell. Then he
meets a lady, Matilda, gathering flowers. Together they walk up a
stream and see a pageant. In this splendid scene, Beatrice appears in
a chariot 'cloaked in green, And living flame the colour of her
gown'.[10] Dante has become united with the love he sought, which
is personal and impersonal, unique and yet universal. Beatrice
reproves him, but also takes him on to an experience he could not
have imagined before, to paradise.

Purgatory: the growth of self-awareness

Purgatory can be viewed as the way of individuation, the search
for becoming who you truly are. Here you work your way through
unconscious material, that which drives you, into conscious

acknowledgement and the understanding awareness of the significance of your life. You have to understand the forces that are your particular bane and problem, and learn and constantly relearn how to transcend them. You have to perceive the unresolved conflicts in yourself and learn how to grow towards greater harmony. You can be led in this journey by glimpses of paradise.

Unlike both hell and paradise, purgatory is in the natural world, and experiences night and day – it is necessary to rest in this struggle, to give place to meditation and restoration, or otherwise you may go backwards. 'Purgatory is the resolute breaking-down, at whatever cost, of the prison walls, so that the soul may be able to emerge at last into liberty and endure unscathed the unveiled light of reality'.[11] As Helen Luke points out, the people in purgatory 'have dared to recognise meaning and to accept responsibility', to search for wholeness.

One large group of those waiting to enter purgatory was that of the 'do-gooders' who had no self-knowledge! None of these had refused the journey like those at the mouth of hell; but they had neglected attention to themselves. We all have an inner journey to take. To enter purgatory it is necessary to ask consciously and to enter knowing you are on a journey.

Much of this work is about the reconciliation and the transcendence of opposites, between which we swing until we have emerged from a particular dualism. Dante and Virgil met various people who explained their situation and the meaning of what was happening to them. A sin which was recognised more in the Middle Ages than the present is that of 'accedie', which is the sin of going along with what is happening, the refusal to stand up for the right, to become who you truly are. This involves standing by whilst evil is done, refusing your own potential, in disillusionment and escapism; we are all to some extent bystanders to terrible things done in our name, or known by us to exist.

To reach the wood on the edge of paradise, to meet Beatrice in love, is to resolve the conflicts within yourself, to be prepared to be happy and whole. It is where the human race could be in all its fullness.

The journey into paradise

Dante and Beatrice then rise up through the planets. The first
three, the moon, Mercury and Venus, lie within the shadow of the
earth. The moon is so near to earth, it is like living in two places at
once. But it is here, when all the things that get in the way have been
swept aside, that you can remember your true identity, and all
striving comes to an end. Mercury is the planet of the leaders, the
way of action – that of people who have achieved much on earth,
but whose successes are tinged with pride. Venus is the planet of the
lovers, but the gift of love may have been misused.

Beyond the shadow of the earth is the sun, the heaven of the
thinkers. Here Dante meets and talks with St Francis, St Thomas and
St Bonaventure. Mars, the next planet, is the way of sacrifice and the
death of the ego, the proud self. Then through to Jupiter, the planet
of the just law and peace givers; and to Saturn, the planet of the
contemplatives, where need and want have disappeared and where
all is seen as it really is. Finally to Gemini, Dante's own sign, where
he meets and is examined by St Peter on faith, hope and love.

Then they come to the Primum Mobile, the still centre of everything in the universe.

> The nature of the universe which stills
> The centre and revolves all else, from here,
> As from its starting point, all movement wills.[12]

Round a point of intense light revolve nine circles, full of angels and
music. This is the source of creation. Dante and Beatrice find themselves in the highest realm of heaven, the Empyrean, a different state
of consciousness, the home of God, where light flows as a river,
surrounded by 'the colours of a wondrous springtime'.[13] Here finally
is the 'Eternal White Rose', the symbol of divine love, beyond both
time and space, thronged with souls. Dante meets St Bernard and
talks with him about this supreme place, and prays. And then come
the famous last lines:

> Here my powers rest from their high fantasy,
> But already I could feel my being turned –
> Instinct and Intellect balanced equally
> As in a wheel whose motion nothing jars
> By the love that moves the Sun and the other stars.[14]

Paradise: discovering love and wisdom

For us the journey through to the heights of paradise can be the realisation more and more truly of both love and knowledge, and that in the end they are the same thing. With the increase in the strength of the soul comes the increase in the ability to face and know things, and love all things as they truly are. It is also uniting one's own uniqueness and hard-gained self-knowledge to the great wholeness and interconnectedness of everything. It is going back home.

Commenting on Francis of Assisi, Helen Luke notes that he personified all his experiences: 'to him Brother Wolf, Sister Water, Brother Pain, Sister Death and "My Lady Poverty" were people to be known and loved personally. Human beings, birds, animals, trees and stones, thoughts and sensations, were all equally alive with meaning: and he lived in immediate personal relatedness with all of them'.[15] Paradise is the knowledge that everything is interconnected, and that we are part of and can personally relate to the whole.

With such insights as 'the greening of the self'[16] we can conceive of ourselves as not just bounded by our own skins, being lonely isolated creatures, but rather as beings potentially in touch with everything. As Joanna Macy writes, 'the way we define and delimit the self is arbitrary. We can place it between our ears and have it looking out from our eyes, or we can widen it to include the air we breathe, or, at other moments, we can cast its boundaries farther to include the oxygen-giving trees and plankton, our external lungs and beyond them, the web of life in which they are sustained'.[17] These two visions, the fourteenth and the twentieth-century visions, contain many of the same things – the sense of the mystery underlying all things, the sense that knowledge is essentially a relationship between the inner self and the world perceived. The inner and the outer worlds are the same thing, space and depth and time are relatively superficial, the deepest and highest reality is the still centre, and all has to be known with love.

THE INSPIRATION OF LOVE

Dante's great message is that the universe is inspired by love and that it is the task of the human soul to search for and unite with that love. The purpose of the universe is to awaken the divine 'I am', the unique and yet universal spirit within all humans – indeed within all creatures. In each one of us, when we are truly realised, the universe is reflected in a unique and inimitable way. Dante in his great journey eventually reaches the 'still centre', the Primum Mobile, in paradise, from which all else revolves, and where our human concepts of time and space no longer apply. 'The still point of the turning world'[18] is found, within himself and within the creation, the space where love and true reality are all and struggles are over. The snow-white rose, original bliss, is at the heart of everything, and the whole of creation is confirmed as unimaginably benign, sublime.

But the journey there is long and hard, through hell and purgatory to paradise. We constantly have to choose whether or not we wish to continue with it, or whether we want to opt out at the many stopping places.

Dante's awakening in his love for Beatrice was the inspiration of his search for love and knowledge and reality. It was the mystical insight that is described by C.S. Lewis in his *Surprised by Joy* or Wordsworth in his 'Ode'.[19] It was the intimation that love and beauty are at the heart of all things, however difficult it is to believe this at many times in our lives. Dante described a vision he had of Beatrice 'in which I beheld things that determined me to speak no more of that blessed one until such time as I could treat of her more worthily';[20] the *Divine Comedy* might be said to be a worthy tribute, a great vision for us all.

8

A perspective on love:
Dame Julian of Norwich
(1342-1413+)

MADELEINE O'CALLAGHAN

It is the year 1394. In the port of Norwich, the second city of England, cargoes from the continent are unloaded on the riverside wharves. Fishing boats bring catches of herring from the North Sea. Norwich is thriving. Despite outbreaks of plague and the disruptions of the Peasants' Revolt some years previously, a brisk commercial energy pervades the city and animates the streets. In the warehouses and merchant premises that line the north bank of the River Wensum, merchants trade in wool, cloth and other goods. Six centuries later, a major restoration project on one of these houses, named Dragon Hall because of some lively wall paintings uncovered in the restoration, will offer the people of late twentieth century Norwich rich insights into the commercial and social life of the fourteenth and fifteenth century city. On the slope that climbs away from the river, a network of small streets is filled with shops and houses supporting and supported by the trade of the port. In one of these streets, minutes from Dragon Hall and the stir of the wharves, people stop at a small window that opens onto the street. They have come to talk to Julian, a woman who for many years has lived as an anchoress in the cell attached to the Church of St Julian.

Norwich is familiar with the anchoritic tradition which led men and women of medieval times to live lives of prayer and contemplation, confined in small cells which were often attached to parish or neighbourhood churches. Connected with the outside world only by a window which opened onto the street, they gave spiritual guidance to those who came looking for support. Caught in a virtually uninterrupted rhythm of prayer, reflection and contemplation, their lives had an intense spiritual force.

LIFE AND CALLING

When we leave aside conjecture and unwarranted assumptions, there is very little that we can know of Julian: a handful of biographical facts gathered from her writings, passing references in the accounts of contemporaries and a few modest bequests naming her as beneficiary. We are not even told her name but know her, as tradition decrees, by the name of the church in Norwich in whose anchorhold she spent most of her life. She was born in 1342, most probably in Norwich, although there is some conjecture, based on her writings, that she may have been born in in Yorkshire.

Life was precarious in mid-fourteenth century England; the Black Death had struck twice in Norwich before Julian was twenty. As a young woman with a spiritual life which was already strong, she prayed with great intensity for a personal experience of God. In May 1373, when she was thirty years old, she received the experience she had longed for. She tells us how she became so seriously ill that she received all the rites of Holy Church. Three days later, her condition had so deteriorated that her curate was called to be present at her death. In this state, weakened by illness and close to death, she had a series of visions, sixteen in all, which she called 'showings' or 'revelations'. These were visions of a loving God revealed in such overwhelming intimacy and power that she chose to withdraw into the anchorhold attached to St Julian's Church, then about 400 years old. Here, supported by one or two women who cared for her material needs (one of them, Sara, is known to us by name), she spent the next twenty years of her life groping towards ways of adequately understanding and expressing her experience of the visions. At the end of that time, in 1393, she rewrote the short account which she had first written down in English shortly after the visions occurred. The new version, known today as the 'Long Text' and published as *The Showings* or *The Revelations of Divine Love,* fills out the original account with extraordinary freshness and clarity, and with a depth and originality of theological reflection that caused Thomas Merton to rank her with Newman as one of the outstanding English theologians. That is all we know. There are no other writings that we know of; no contemporary manuscripts of the *Showings.* The date of her death is uncertain though we know that she was 'still alive',[1] as the introduction to the *Showings* tells us, in Norwich in 1413 when she would have been seventy-one.

Julian has little interest in telling us about herself. She quietly and consistently shifts the focus of our gaze away from herself and towards the revelations which formed the pivotal moment of her life. She is self-deprecating when speaking of herself, referring to herself as 'a simple, unlettered creature',[2] 'a woman, ignorant, weak and frail'.[3] The modesty of these descriptions is contradicted by the facts. While she may not have known Latin, the accepted language for theological writing in her time, she writes with clarity and vigour, with a strong, distinctive voice. As the first woman known to have written in English, she is the forerunner of all the great women writers of English literature. Her writings are evidence that she was neither feeble nor frail and these descriptions of herself can be best understood in the light of the virtual disregard for the validity of women's spiritual experience in the England of her time. A contemporary account tells of another woman of East Anglia, Margery Kempe of King's Lynn, who asked the priest, Richard of Caistor, to receive her for a few hours one afternoon to discuss with her the mystery of the love of God. Richard's response was dismissive. He refused to receive her, on the grounds that it was impossible that a woman should have adequate spiritual resources to sustain a theological discussion, even for an hour or two. Indeed he vowed never to eat meat again if he found that she could sustain the topic even for one hour.

In this climate, when it was still possible for women to be severely punished, even killed, for speaking out on theological matters, Julian needed to be circumspect. Deeply moved by her revelations and the urge to make their message of God's love and compassion known to her fellow-Christians, she would have been careful to ensure that she was not silenced by churchmen. She walked this narrow and potentially dangerous path light-footedly, with skill and good humour. She consistently submits herself to her 'Mother, Holy Church as a simple child should',[4] while at the same time firmly asserting what she has experienced in her own encounter with God. A favourite device of hers is to invoke ecclesiastical authority with unquestioning and undoubtedly sincere affirmations of assent and to juxtapose with these statements the insights which her visions have given her. 'For I know by the ordinary teaching of Holy Church, and by my own feeling, that the blame of our sins hangs continually on us. This then, was my astonishment, that I saw our Lord God showing no more blame to us than if we were as pure and as holy as the angels are in heaven'.[5] Because God's is the higher judgement, revealed personally to her, she feels compelled to accept it. Elsewhere she adds: 'I believe and understand the ministration of holy angels, as scholars tell, but it was not revealed to me. For God is nearest and meekest, highest and lowest and he does everything ... all that we need'.[6] Again and again, by implication or directly, she affirms the validity of her own experience and the primary obligation of conscience to mediate God when that is what God asks. 'Because I am a woman, ought I therefore to believe that I ought not to tell you about the goodness of God, when I saw at that same time that it is his will that it be known'.[7] A woman of robustly independent judgement, her need is always to experience on her own account; to learn and to understand from that experience.

A WINDOW TO THE WORLD

This is the woman to whose window the people of Norwich came with the dilemmas of their lives and their spiritual needs. It is not difficult to imagine why they were drawn to her and how her compassion, joyfulness and the spiritual wisdom laid down in twenty years of consistent inner exploration restored them to a sense of God's love for them and of their own worth. It would have been difficult for these men and women to conceive of a time, six centuries later, when Norwich would be known, at least for some people, not so much for its impact as a vital commercial centre but for the personality and writing of this hidden woman who, enclosed in her cell, created a still centre at the heart of a bustling city. For, after six hundred years of virtual obscurity, Julian's cell, reconstructed after war damage, has once again become a place of pilgrimage. A rediscovered Julian has emerged to become a prophet for our age; opening new windows for us, expanding our consciousness of what it is to be human beings, offering us insights into the nature and identity of God and our relationship with the Divine.

At first glance she seems remote from contemporary consciousness. She was a woman of her age and six hundred years of change separate us from her. Some of her descriptions, some aspects of her spiritual experience, strike a jarring, alien note. Her choice of lifestyle seems extreme, not to say bizarre. Immured in her small cell, is she not just another example of a neurotic, life-denying religious fanatic? Her writings are too filled with common sense to allow that accusation to be sustained for very long. Stereotypical images of the mystic rapt in a perpetual state of ecstasy are debunked by her earthiness. While she does experience extraordinary states of intimacy with God, for her the spiritual path is as much concerned with 'digging and ditching, and sweating and turning the soil; over and over'[8] as with esoteric states. Our task is 'to dig deep down, and to water the plants at the proper times'.[9] Her images are of everyday things: the scales on a herring, rain dripping from the eaves, a child's ABC, a sweat-encrusted shirt, a man sending his servant on a journey. One of the most endearing aspects of her personality is her love of merriment and a laughter which is so infectious that it sets everybody laughing.

A WINDOW TO THE SPIRIT

In addition to the window which connected her to the outside world, Julian's cell would have had two other windows. One linked her to the small support group who cared for her daily needs. The other opened to the church, enabling her to participate in the Mass and Divine Offices. This window, opening, as it were, to the world of the spirit, is an effective symbol of Julian's primary focus: God, her loving creator. The pattern of her life is a living out of this relationship. From the beginning she longs for an intense experience of God. In the second chapter of the *Revelations* where she tells us of the background of her showings, the word 'desire' appears over twelve times in connection with the three gifts she had prayed for. When she receives the encounter with God which she had longed for, she is totally open to it. While merriment, joy and delight are integral to her experience of God, it also involves suffering. The visions themselves are accompanied by psychic and physical pain and a near death experience, all of which she accepts unquestioningly, as part of a necessary process. She chooses a lifestyle in which she can reflect on the momentous impact of her showings. In the role of anchoress, a way of life widely practised in contemporary spiritual culture, she finds an environment where she can explore the full meaning of her experience of God while at the same time caring for the needs of the people. Her writings are filled with longing for full understanding; for more complete experience and fuller knowledge. To paraphrase the words of T.S. Eliot, some of whose poems would be influenced by her writings six centuries later, she never ceases from exploration. Given this passion for learning and understanding, a period of twenty years does not seem quite so long a time to spend in assimilating a major spiritual experience. At the end of this time, when her journey into the meaning of her showings is completed, she offers us a book filled with wisdom and love which continues, after six hundred years, to be a source of hope and comfort. Seen in this light, her life is a work of profound compassion. We may not choose to live as she did, but her spiritual path, with its processes of longing, openness to experience, integration and compassion offers us a way of wisdom, integration and wholeness for our own spiritual journey.

IMAGES OF GOD

The compassion for her fellow humans which compels Julian to write is expressed in many other ways. In particular, she offers us, out of her contemplation of her showings, compassionate insight into the nature of the divine. Images of God as remote, punishing, harsh, vindictive, a divine accountant carefully balancing the books, bear no resemblance to the God of her revelations. Her vision of a God of love offers a very different perspective. Loving, wise, tender, compassionate, understanding, energising, joyful and merry, the God of her encounters is a God of life, love and light. One of the most remarkable aspects of Julian's writings, as of those of other mystics who mediate to us a personal experience of the divine, is the immediacy and impact of those moments when she relays God's words directly, in the first person. God reveals some of the richness and complexity of his identity in direct conversation with her: 'I am ... the power and goodness of fatherhood; I am ... the wisdom and lovingness of motherhood; I am ... the light and grace which is all blessed love; ... the supreme goodness of every kind of thing'.[10] This insight into the feminine aspect of the Divine is among Julian's most radical contributions to the expansion of theological consciousness. She presents it to us as a self-evident fact, bluntly, without preamble or excuse. 'God almighty is our loving Father, and God all wisdom is our loving Mother'.[11] She devotes a number of chapters to developing this theme: an indication of its importance to her. Motherhood and fatherhood; the feminine and masculine are expressions of a divinity who incorporates and transcends both of these, and all other created realities.

In Julian's *Showings* we meet a God whose essence is goodness and whose motivating energy, in creating the universe, is love spilling out of that goodness. In her understanding everything comes into being out of the love of God who established the universe out of love and continues, with that same love, to preserve it in being. Creation is inherently good. Far from despising it, God holds the whole in being as blithely, lightly and tenderly as a hazelnut held in the palm of the hand. This sacredness of creation is implicit in all that Julian tells us about God. It is difficult to separate the two. In her account of the death of Christ she tells us that natural cataclysms in the heavens and on earth accompanied this event because of the inherent connection between the divine and nature. In telling us that God is 'eveything that is good',[12] Julian does no more than reiterate a truth insisted on by all theologians. But when she continues, 'and the goodness that everything possesses is God's',[13] (in short, saying that when we experience goodness we experience God), then she offers us a startling and necessary reminder of the true nature of reality. Julian's writings are saturated with the experience of God's immanence. God is integrated with everything. One of her more emphatic passages hammers this home: 'See, I am God. See, I am in all things. See, I do all things. See, I never remove my hands from my works nor ever shall'.[14]

GOD IN RELATIONSHIP

In Julian's world then, it is virtually impossible to talk about God without talking about God in relationship. If God is immanent in all of creation, it follows inevitably that the divine is totally implicated in the life of the human and vice versa. She finds no difference between God and our being; everything has being in God. In image after image she tries to bring home to us the intimacy of mutual presence between ourselves and God. God is 'our lover';[15] 'the foundation on which our soul stands';[16] 'our true spouse'.[17] One of her most homely and comforting images represents God as wrapping us round: 'our clothing who wraps and enfolds us for love', who 'embraces and shelters us'.[18] Julian is trying to bring home to us our total significance and value; to help us experience ourselves as blessed, as loved, as wrapped round with tenderness by God; as the source of God's pleasure and delight. In creating the human, God 'made our soul as beautiful, as good, as precious a creature'[19] as could be made. Not only does God delight in this precious human creature, addressing her/him tenderly as 'My dear darling',[20] but God longs for a response. He is thirsty for us, longing for a relationship of mutuality and oneness. This longing of God for us evokes our own natural longing for him. Julian, like Augustine of Hippo, comments on how this desire leaves us unsettled and seeking rest where there is no rest, until we can be totally at one with God. As Julian has already repeatedly referred to God as present within us from the beginning and holding us in being, what she seems to be emphasising here is the necessary process of coming to consciousness and a full acceptance of our oneness with God. The true identity of our being is identity with God. The whole purpose of our life is to keep seeking until we know God and ourselves truly and enter into the fullness of our identity with him.

Our longing for oneness with the divine draws us more and more deeply into our own humanity. For Julian, the spiritual journey of the human involves entering into our incarnation as completely as Christ did. Every aspect of our humanity is sacred: the body is as integral to our being as the soul. For her, God's courtesy and care are expressed in every aspect of our body's functioning. 'A man walks upright and the food in his body is shut in as in a well-made purse. When the time of necessity comes, the purse is opened, then shut again in a most seemly fashion – for God does not despise what he has made'.[21] Julian is a stranger to dualism; in her world everything is interconnected and interdependent. 'For as the body is clad in the cloth and the flesh in the skin and the bones in the flesh, and the heart in the trunk, so are we soul and body, clad and enclosed in the goodness of God'.[22] Her anticipation of what heaven will be like is expressed in gloriously sensuous language: it will be an experience of seeing, feeling, smelling, tasting God.

SUFFERING: PROBLEMS OF EVIL

Given this groundedness in the goodness of a loving God who longs for us, how do we deal with the presence of evil, with our own damaging tendencies and the sinfulness that has been such a focus of Christian spiritual writers over the centuries? The problem of evil and pain preoccupies Julian. She herself had suffered acutely in her illness; had witnessed in Norwich the horrific effects of the Black Death. Through those who came to her anchorhold for help, she knew the sufferings of the poor, exacerbated by wars and excessive taxation. Sin is a vivid and terrible reality, deserving of blame and wrath. Yet, in her showings she can find no trace of an angry response from God who insists that 'all shall be well'.[23] Typically she asks bluntly for an explanation of this anomaly, demanding to know how all can be well when sin is so harmful to humankind. While she receives no fully satisfactory answer, the conclusion she draws is rooted in compassion, the compassion of a God who created humans in love. It is found in Chapter 51 of the *Long Text,* in her parable of the master and the servant, a story which epitomises the tender, 'courteous' God of Julian's revelations. The servant, on an errand for the master, falls into a ravine and cannot extricate himself, remaining separated from his master. This separation is caused, not by the master's anger at the servant's fall but by the servant's inability to turn and look at the master; his inability to receive the master's love and appreciation of him. The real pain of sin is not so much a matter of what we do wrong, the failings which are inevitable in the human condition, as in the resulting alienation from our true selves and from God. As God is incapable of anger (the wrath, she tells us, is all on our side) and does not blame us, it is self-defeating for us to blame ourselves unduly. For Julian, too much mourning and focus on sin is against the true order of things. So, we are to acknowledge that we are human and make mistakes and should not demand of ourselves a state of perfection that God does not demand. Here, as in all her teaching, she presents to us a God whose being is love and compassion and whose deepest desire is to restore us to an awareness of mutual connection and relationship.

THE RETURN TO LOVE

So, as always, with Julian, we come back to love. At the end of her *Revelations,* in the very last chapter, she tells us how, for fifteen years, with typical tenacity, she had continually asked for an understanding of the essential meaning of her revelations. Finally the answer comes: 'Would you know your Lord's meaning in this ? Learn it well. Love was his meaning. Who showed it you? Love. What did he show you? Love. Why did he show it you? For love. Hold fast to this'.[24]

Holding fast, then, to this basic vision of a world created out of love and held in being by a loving God who delights in his creation, we can, like the people of Norwich, continue to come to Julian's window. From here, she offers us new perspectives and a wisdom which can help us move with grace and her favourite 'courtesy' into a future of greater wholeness and more harmonious relationship with God and creation.

PART THREE

The Modern Quest

9

The poet as mystic:
Thomas Hardy
(1840-1928)

DAVID HASLETT

nyone who has attempted to write creatively will know the strange exhilaration of the experience when, after frustrations and creative blocks, one finds oneself unexpectedly transformed in a way akin to possession and words come spilling out from hitherto hidden sources. And re-reading in the more sober light of the following day, the writer may often ask, wonderingly, 'Did I write that?' and question the source of the inspiration.

Inspiration, that word links the poet and the mystic as each attempts to give voice to the inexpressible. Deep religious experience leads the person fortunate enough to have been transported to an awareness of a reality beyond the mundane, to grasp at words to express the nature of that reality. In approaching the works of great writers all of us can glimpse the transported state of the mystic if we will, even if few attain to the state of genius or find the power with words to become outstanding poets. It is the poets among us who come closest to being able to say the unsayable. Poetry distils experience and to do so it forces words out of the commonplace mode we employ in everyday discourse and obliquely hints at a realm of experience that many of us aspire to enter.

There is a long and immensely rich tradition of religious poetry and the works of poets such as George Herbert[1] and Gerard Manley Hopkins[2] have often proved to be invaluable aids as we each make our spiritual journey. These poets provide us with an intensity of experience which can often help us to measure our own progress and lead us into an ever richer appreciation of the world we live in, the place of the spiritual within it, and our relation to it. They wrote from a specifically Christian viewpoint which is hardly surprising as both men were priests, Herbert an Anglican and Hopkins a Jesuit. Thomas Hardy, however, was in no sense conventionally religious, indeed his attitude to organised religion was fairly hostile, but he nonetheless articulates something of the creation spirit. This chapter explores some of his poetry. He is still probably best known as a novelist though he began and ended his writing career as a poet.

POET OF THE FIELDS

Hardy's work differs markedly from that of his early contemporaries. The work of the major poets of the Victorian era, Tennyson and Browning, has an air of being addressed to an educated, middle class public. There is a sense of the poet seeing himself as having a public role to play. Hardy's early poetry seems small scale and intimate by comparison and this undoubtedly owes something to his background and upbringing. There is no whiff of the literary salon about his work! He was born in Higher Bockhampton in rural Dorset in 1840 and was educated in local schools. His father, a stonemason, apprenticed him at an early age to a local architect engaged in restoring old churches. From 1862 until 1867 Hardy worked for an architect in London and later practised in his native Dorset. His early attempts at poetry met with little success and he turned to the writing of novels. By the mid 1870s he was able to support himself through his writing. After an outcry (led by a number of Anglican bishops) over the supposed immorality of his last novel, *Jude the Obscure,*[3] he devoted himself to poetry for the last thirty years of his life. By the time of his death in 1928 he was firmly established as both a great novelist and a great poet, having produced approximately one thousand poems.

That is a considerable body of work and one which can prove daunting to the newcomer. Where does one start? Here are sonnets and ballads, long narrative poems, philosophical poems, war poems and poems about national events like the sinking of the Titanic. The discussion which follows concentrates mainly on those poems of Hardy which the English composer Benjamin Britten[4] set to music in his song cycle 'Winter Words'. After all, as T.S. Eliot[5] commented, 'poetry aspires to the condition of music'. These settings by Britten provide us with an entry to Hardy's world and, for music lovers, probably enrich the experience. Certainly we have the coming together of two great humanists who share an equivocal view of organised religion but who articulate a concern for the fate of humanity.

THE LOSS OF EDEN

Hardy's world view is generally described as pessimistic. The characters who people his novels and poems are often the victims of cruel chance. If a deity exists at all, it is often seen as indifferent at best to human suffering. At the end of his novel *Tess of the d'Urbervilles* we are informed that 'the President of the Immortals ... had ended his sport with Tess',[6] making that deity sound like the chair of some nightmarish bureaucracy. Religion brings no comfort and is characterised as pharisaic and unsympathetic. The clergyman in the poem 'The Choirmaster's Burial', who refuses a last request for music at the graveside, is entirely typical:

> 'I think,' said the vicar,
> 'A read service quicker
> Than viols out-of-doors
> In these frosts and hoars.
> That old-fashioned way
> Requires a fine day,
> And it seems to me
> It had better not be.'[7]

The easy rhymes set the smooth autocrat unerringly before us. Interestingly, Hardy grants the dead choirmaster his musical tribute from a supernatural source:

> ...a band all in white
> Like the saints in church-glass,
> Singing and playing...

which the selfish vicar observes at the dead of night. Here, at least,
God is generous even if his ministers are not. Unfortunately, we are
not granted a glimpse of the vicar's reaction to this divine reproof! It
is important to emphasise, however, that Hardy was a writer who
came to maturity at a time of great crisis for the church and for
humanity. The devastating effect that Darwin's[8] theories had on
fundamentalist religious belief in the latter part of the nineteenth
century is most powerfully dealt with in Edmund Gosse's book
Father and Son.[9] Matthew Arnold's[10] poem, 'Dover Beach', written
within a decade of the appearance of *On the Origin of Species*,
provides us with a contemporaneous poetic response:

> ...The Sea of Faith
> Was once, too, at the full, and round earth's shore
> Lay like the folds of a bright girdle furl'd.
> But now I only hear
> Its melancholy, long, withdrawing roar,
> Retreating, to the breath
> Of the night-wind, down the vast edges drear
> And naked shingles of the world...[11]

For Arnold the only hope in a meaningless world of pain and
suffering resides in human love.

At first glance Hardy seems similarly pessimistic. In 'The Oxen',
perhaps his most famous poem, and certainly the most frequently
anthologised (ironically often in volumes of religious verse), Hardy
deals with the desire to believe in the Christian story, but also, by
implication, the impossibility of doing so, at least in any literal sense.
It refers to a folk belief that the animal kingdom would fall on its
knees at midnight on Christmas Eve in spontaneous adoration at the
birth of Christ. It is worth pausing with this poem for a moment as
it so clearly displays Hardy's attitude to what we categorise as 'religion':

> Christmas Eve, and twelve of the clock.
> 'Now they are all on their knees,'
> An elder said as we sat in a flock
> By the embers in hearthside ease.

> We pictured the meek mild creatures where
>   They dwelt in their strawy pen,
> Nor did it occur to one of us there
>   To doubt they were kneeling then.
>
> So fair a fancy few would weave
>   In these years! Yet, I feel,
> If someone said on Christmas Eve,
>   'Come; see the oxen kneel
>
> 'In the lonely barton by yonder coomb
>   Our childhood used to know,'
> I should go with him in the gloom,
>   Hoping it might be so.[12]

It exhibits many of the qualities we come to expect in a poem by Hardy – the naturalness of the diction, the concision of the form, the slight melancholy of the tone. The contrast between 'then' and 'now' is emphasised by the contrasts between the first two stanzas and the last two. There is an easy flow about the beginning, an inevitability about the rhymes which suggests a happy and contented community, secure and united in faith. This is quickly broken up in the third stanza where the awkward alliteration puts an end to the flow. Suddenly the thought is more complex, and so is its articulation. We stumble over the lines, we are no longer supported by rhythm and syntax as we originally were. This is a poem about the death of certainty and with it, the fragmentation of community – notice that the 'elder' sitting among a 'flock' of people is replaced by the anonymous and solitary 'someone'; thus we have lost not only the certainty of belief but are also divided from each other because of it. Darwin's own faith faltered not so much because of his scientific discoveries, but because of the irrationality and injustice of Victorian fundamentalism. The artists and writers who created in his shadow obviously had greater difficulties.

THE SPIRITUAL SEARCH

Yet it is impossible to read Hardy's work without realising that there is a profound religious spirit at work, albeit not of the kind that would have been recognised as such by many of his contemporaries. He remained essentially a countryman all his life and a sense of landscape and the natural world is one of the most striking characteristics of his work. The destruction of an agricultural past and its replacement with a brutalised, materialistic, urban way of life is seen as soul destroying. It sets us at odds not only with each other but also with the whole world of nature. Yet there is nothing sentimental or naive in Hardy's view of nature. Take, for example, 'Proud Songsters':

> The thrushes sing as the sun is going,
> And the finches whistle in ones and pairs,
> And as it gets dark loud nightingales
> In bushes
> Pipe, as they can when April wears,
> As if all Time were theirs.
>
> These are brand new birds of twelve-months' growing,
> Which a year ago, or less than twain,
> No finches were, nor nightingales,
> Nor thrushes,
> But only particles of grain,
> And earth, and air, and rain.[13]

Hardy's diction is characteristically direct and unpretentious so that the most cursory reading of this yields a meaning – it is a poem which clearly delights in the miracle of creation. A closer examination with a consideration of the implications of its form yields much more. One of the most striking features of Hardy's poetry is its multiplicity of forms. Of course, many of his poems make use of standard forms such as the sonnet or ballad but when one considers those poems which are not formulaic, one is astonished by the diversity of form. There is very little duplication throughout his large body of work and the form of this poem is wholly unique. This should alert us to the importance Hardy attaches to this technical aspect of the poem. Its very layout on the page suggests the physical darting and swooping of the birds (note the unexpectedly short fourth line). Moreover, the rhyme scheme is strangely elusive. There are four lines without a rhyme of any kind and we might well wonder whether one will ever appear and then, suddenly, the last two lines of the stanza not only rhyme with each other but also, in an unexpected doubling back effect, with the second line. It has the effect of making us catch our breath, but before we have time to recover from that, the first line of the second stanza equally surprisingly rhymes with the opening line of the poem. There is a sense of the piece being laced together.

The form of the second stanza then proceeds to emulate the scheme of the first although new rhymes prevent any feeling of sameness. On one level this to-ing and fro-ing of rhymes is wonderfully illustrative of the movements of the birds but it goes beyond that. An impression of breathlessness is certainly created but it also shows that beneath the seeming randomness of the poem there is an underlying strength of design, and the poem is meticulously controlled. So too in creation, where all may seem chaotic and arbitrary, where we may be oblivious of the design, it is there all the same, underpinning existence.[14] Notice also how the vowel sounds expand in the second stanza ('twain', 'grain', 'rain') as the poem moves from simple concrete observation to a more philosophical view, ending as it spins into the infinity of the ever-repeating cycle of life and death. The repeated 'ands' of the last line serve to give emphasis to the elements which constitute our being and also the essential simplicity and facility of God's great design.

Humankind is conspicuously absent in this poem. Hardy often describes the world of nature before our 'ecological fall'. For Hardy, we are all time-haunted, unlike the birds who exist in the here and now ('as if all Time were theirs'). As Hamlet mused, our ability to look 'before and after', that is to project into the future and remember the past, may be the single thing that separates us from the rest of the animal kingdom and causes us most unhappiness. We are denied the simple pleasures of the birds, or is it that we have come to deny ourselves these pleasures? Hardy, like the mystic, implies that we need to abandon our rational, intellectual selves and simply Be. We are at odds with the natural world, set apart from it and consequently unhappy, a point very succinctly summed up in 'Wagtail and Baby':

> A baby watched a ford, whereto
> A wagtail came for drinking;
> A blaring bull went wading through,
> The wagtail showed no shrinking.

A stallion splashed his way across,
The birdie nearly sinking;
He gave his plumes a twitch and toss,
And held his own unblinking.

Next saw the baby round the spot
A mongrel slowly slinking;
The wagtail gazed, but faltered not
In dip and sip and prinking.

A perfect gentleman then neared;
The wagtail, in a winking,
With terror rose and disappeared;
The baby fell a-thinking.[15]

There is a very nice contrast here between some of the more bois-
terous aspects of the animal kingdom – the blaring bull, the splashing
stallion and the mongrel – with an impressive representative of
humanity – a 'perfect gentleman'. It appears that there is a unity in
the animal kingdom from which humans have excluded themselves.
All animals, like the aged bird in 'The Darkling Thrush',[16] (another
of Hardy's most frequently anthologised poems), are privy to a secret
of the universe that we, as humans, have lost. Not quite all of us,
however, as the baby is in harmony with the world around it. The
implication is that we must retain the view of the child if we are to
avoid this division. Adult consciousness seems to rob us of our innocence and pitch us into suffering. Far from being born in a state of
original sin, Hardy infers that we acquire it as we mature. In one of
his most powerful poems, 'Before Life and After', he examines this
aspect of human pain:

A time there was – as one may guess
And as, indeed, earth's testimonies tell –
Before the birth of consciousness,
When all went well.

None suffered sickness, love, or loss,
None knew regret, starved hope, or heart-burnings,
None cared whatever crash or cross
Brought wrack to things.

If something ceased, no tongue bewailed,
If something winced and waned, no heart was wrung;

If brightness dimmed, and dark prevailed,
No sense was stung.

But the disease of feeling germed,
And primal rightness took the tinct of wrong;
Ere nescience shall be reaffirmed
How long, how long?[17]

From the very beginning of this poem we are unsettled – the syntax is awkward, turning in on itself as Hardy struggles to articulate a complex notion. Yet, in marked contrast to what has preceded it, the last line of the first stanza has a beautiful simplicity. Then the poem moves uneasily between a strange juxtaposition of positives and negatives ('none... none... none...' 'if... no...'). If we are unsure exactly what is being said, if we have to struggle to resolve these ambiguities, then that is surely Hardy's intention – the world we find ourselves in does not admit of easy answers and humanity is certainly not at ease. We struggle to master the world through our developed rational minds yet we are not fully in control as the word "winced" shows, with its connotation of involuntary pulling back from physical as well as mental pain. Hardy is conjuring up a world where we used to be insensible to all those things which cause present distress – ironically, the poet has to do so from a position of present knowledge, yet the desperate longing for a world of ignorance is ultimately the theme of the poem. If only we had the capability of the great religious mystics to escape into a different realm of consciousness!

The last stanza makes clear what has gone wrong – 'the disease of feeling germed'. What a startlingly ambiguous word 'germed' is in this context, conveying simultaneously growth and its opposite, decay and corruption! Thus we have moved from a state of original blessing to a world of 'wrong', where we have lost our way. We may long for a state of unknowing, of ignorance and naivety, but we cannot undo the past and humanity is left to make the best of it. What, then, is the way forward? We must surely enter the darkness for it is 'in a dark time the eye begins to see', as the American poet Roethke has noted.

Hardy's poetry is full of examples of positive thinking, generally when he is writing about the wonders of creation and the unity of all created things. Humankind is divided from this and in numerous bleak poems he explores our separateness from the rest of creation. It is his willingness to look clearly and unflinchingly at the darker aspects of life that has led to the common view of his art as pessimistic. However, he is also much concerned with the transforming power of compassion and creative thinking, and is especially strong on showing us the world through the uncorrupted eyes of a child. The child has not yet learned to control the world through so-called rational or intellectual processes but rather through instinct:

At the Railway Station, Upway

'There is not much that I can do,
For I've no money that's quite my own!'
Spoke up the pitying child –
A little boy with a violin
At the station before the train came in, –
'But I can play my fiddle to you,
And a nice one 'tis, and good in tone!'

The man in the handcuffs smiled;
The constable looked and he smiled, too,
As the fiddle began to twang;
And the man in the handcuffs suddenly sang
With grimful glee:
'This life so free
Is the thing for me!'
And the constable smiled, and said no word,
As if unconscious of what he heard;
And so they went on till the train came in –
The convict, and boy with the violin.[18]

Like so many of Hardy's poems, this resembles a short story in its delineation of what James Joyce called an 'epiphany', that is a spiritual manifestation, a single moment which reveals a world. The situation is revealed to us gradually as we do not know initially what it is that has evoked the child's pity. That is because it is of no consequence to him. He has not yet learned to judge and condemn. Pathetically, he seems to believe that material resources are called for but lacking those, he offers his art. It is typical of Hardy that the convict should join in the tune with words of such bitter irony (and note how the tightness of the rhyme scheme at that point emphasises the irony by imprisoning the sentiment). The artlessness of the boy's art, his creativity, his 'nescience' – of the crime, of the criminal, of the conventional indifference to an everyday scene like this these transform the situation. Even the constable, presumably hitherto inflexible and unbending, permits himself a smile, though otherwise he maintains his aloofness. Suddenly the mundane event is illuminated and humanised.

THE SEER IN THE MIST

Hardy was writing at a time when the certainties of centuries seemed to have been lost irrevocably. He sees humankind as set on a lonely pinnacle, confused and uncertain about how to proceed, divided from the natural world yet longing for unity with it. He invites us to look at these divisions with him, to face them and to struggle to reconcile them. He offers no easy solutions, and his world is not a comfortable one. His message is more pressingly urgent today than it was when he was writing. Yet it is too simplistic to characterise him as morbid, cynical and pessimistic. His poems are often lit up with sly shafts of humour and he is ever alive to the ironies which abound. And for a writer who lived much of his life in the nineteenth century, he is often surprisingly modern in his outlook. Take for example this extract from 'A Philosophical Fantasy' where he engages in a dialogue with God:

> ...I ask you, Sir or Madam,
> (I know no more than Adam,
> Even vaguely, what your sex is, –
> Though feminine I had thought you
> Till seers as 'Sire' besought you...)[19]

Hardy, like Dame Julian of Norwich, knows that the Godhead is too large, too removed from our simplistic thinking, to be contained by gender!

10

The evolving creation:
Charles Darwin
(1809-1882)
and
Pierre Teilhard de Chardin
(1881-1955)

MARTIN COUNIHAN

C harles Robert Darwin was born in 1809, and in 1859
published *The Origin of Species by Means of Natural Selection,
or the Preservation of Favoured Races in the Struggle for Life*, to
give his best-known book its full title. Midway through the inter-
vening years Darwin undertook an extraordinary and life-changing
voyage around the world, visiting some of the most exotic and
remote parts of the globe aboard HMS *Beagle* from 1831 to 1836. He
also made a personal inner journey, no less difficult in its own way,
from being a student of theology and would-be ordinand to an
agnosticism verging on atheism. Nevertheless the 'Devil's Chaplain'
was buried on 26 April 1882 amid great pomp in Westminster
Abbey. He had brought the world face to face with the implications
of a theory of evolution according to which the future is created
only from what is here with us in the present.

Pierre Teilhard de Chardin was born in 1881 in the Auvergne. He
had a Jesuit education, joined the Order, and remained faithful to it

until his death in 1955. His early writings exhibited in embryonic form most of the dominant themes of his later work. He was a palaeontologist and theologian, and integrated the ideas of evolution and continuous creation. He held that the appearance of humans in the evolutionary process introduced the element of self-consciousness. This imposed upon the biosphere a new realm of evolutionary development, the 'noosphere', or the world of conscious thought. In his vision, humanity recreates itself and is eventually to be fulfilled in the attainment of a universal cosmic destiny, the 'Omega Point'. Teilhard's superiors were worried by the novelty of his ideas, and consequently he was unable to publish his work or to accept academic posts as freely as he might.

The rise of Darwinism led to many misunderstandings and various confused reactions; some took it as a final breach between science and religion. Some misused it to justify atheism and racism. Even today, many find it hard to reconcile the theory of evolution with any spirituality of creation. The importance of Pierre Teilhard de Chardin lies in his showing, by the example of his own spiritual journey, that Christianity and the theory of evolution can be understood to describe the same process and the same future.[1]

THE THEORY OF EVOLUTION

From the late seventeenth century to the early nineteenth century a tradition of 'natural theology' flourished in England, where the wonders of nature were seen as evidence for the existence and beneficence of the creator. It was generally accepted that the species of animals and plants were all created together and were fixed. No genetic relationship was imagined between different species. In particular, humans were not considered to be related to any other earthly creatures. Alternative ideas began to gain prominence only towards the end of the eighteenth century and in the early years of the nineteenth. In France, Georges Louis Leclerc, the Comte de Buffon, suggested that apes might be degenerate descendants of humans; and Jean-Baptiste de Lamarck developed a theory of the evolution of one species from another by the inheritance of characteristics acquired during life, by the 'use and disuse' of organs, limbs, mental faculties and so on. A well-known evolutionist at the end of the eighteenth century was Erasmus Darwin, the grandfather of Charles Darwin.

The theory of evolution involves the observation that all species can reproduce at a much greater rate than would be necessary to maintain constant populations. But populations in practice remain more or less constant. Therefore, many individuals of every species must fail to achieve adulthood and to breed. There must be a struggle for life, as a result of which only the exceptional individual survives long enough to reproduce successfully. Given that there is competition for life, which individuals will be successful? There are variations among the individuals belonging to any species. In any given circumstances, this means that some individuals will be more fitted to survive than others by virtue of their particular characteristics. They will have a competitive edge over others. Consequently, over many generations the structure of a population may shift, with 'favoured' characteristics becoming more prevalent. In this way, species can change over long periods of time. The characteristics favoured depend on the environment in which a particular population of the species finds itself, and on the particular ecological niche that a subpopulation has chosen to exploit. Consequently, a range of environments and of niches can lead from one species to a range of species over a period of time. This is the 'origin of species'.

Charles Darwin[2] developed the theory into an explanation of the origin of all animals and plants. He believed that 'animals have descended from at most only four or five progenitors, and plants from an equal or lesser number' and inferred that 'probably all the organic beings that ever lived on this earth have descended from some one primordial form, into which life was first breathed'.[3]

In *The Origin of Species,* Darwin says practically nothing explicitly about humanity, restricting his discussion to non-human animals and plants. However, near the end of the book he speculates about evolution in a human context. He foresaw future research demonstrating the gradual acquisition of mental powers and throwing light on human history.[4]

One of the most striking images presented by Darwin is that of a 'family tree' of all life:

As buds give rise by growth to fresh buds, and these, if vigorous,
branch out and overtop on all sides many a feebler branch, so by
generation I believe it has been with the great Tree of Life,
which fills with its dead and broken branches the crust of the
earth, and covers the surface with its ever-branching and beautiful ramifications.[5]

This image is an inversion of the traditional downward-spreading
family tree. Human generations have been imagined as branching
down from distinguished ancestors, founders of dynasties and
nations, and ultimately from gods. In Jewish tradition, adopted
widely in the Christian world, the divine ancestor was replaced by
Adam, quasi-divine forerunner ('type') of Christ, excluded
temporarily from paradise. Deep in western mythology is the idea
that we are descended from our betters. Darwin reversed this.
Although his later book on human evolution, published in 1871, was
entitled *The Descent of Man,* Darwin actually replaced a descent with
an ascent: instead of descending from heaven, humanity rose from
the slime; instead of gods, our ancestors were beasts.

The theory of evolution was taken to imply that the ascent of
humanity was not guided by any divine hand; the process of evolution is directionless; and it is negative, depending on the elimination
of those less fitted to the struggle for life, not on the moral superi-
ority of the survivors. There was no pre-selection, no destiny that
called us forward. Not only were our ancestors 'beasts', they were
not even intrinsically 'better beasts'. The theory of evolution
demoted humanity. This contrasted strongly with the traditional
human-centred imagery in, for example, the eighth Psalm, where
the human being is seen as 'little less than a god' and crowned 'with
glory and splendour'.[6]

RESPONSES TO DARWINISM

Darwin's theory of evolution evoked a number of different
responses. There was the despair which cries out from much of the
poetry of the time, lamenting the loss of faith and of innocence. The
poets reached out to embrace nature with a new melancholy deeply
etched with pessimism. This has been seen in Thomas Hardy's
poetry in the previous chapter. The mood is especially marked in

parts of Tennyson's 'In Memoriam',[7] Hopkins' 'Nondum',[8] and most bleakly in Matthew Arnold's 'Dover Beach'.[9]

The history of ninetenth century Darwinism in England is often presented as a battle between science and religion. From that point of view, the poets express the bewilderment and impotence of Christianity, confounded in the face of the new scientific reality. But it is possible to argue a convincing case that this battle between science and religion was a deliberately fostered illusion put about by a small but influential group of scientists whose aim was to transfer power from the Church to the emerging Victorian scientific establishment. The conspicuous public controversy between churchmen and evolutionists was artificially fomented. There is no intrinsic contradiction between Christianity and the theory of evolution.[10]

Although Charles Darwin himself lost his Christian faith, he claims to have done so for reasons not directly to do with the theory of evolution. In his autobiography he explains how he was repelled by the 'manifestly false history of the world' in the Old Testament, and by a faith that attributed to God 'the feelings of a revengeful tyrant',[11] waiting to cast unbelievers into hell, including his father, brother, and best friends.[12] So the tension in Darwin's own mind lay not between the theory of evolution and orthodox Christianity but between rationalism and a literal interpretation of the Bible. Darwin, then, rejects Christianity for what today would be regarded as the wrong reasons: a doctrine of eternal damnation which was being heavily overemphasised in Victorian times and is inessential to Christianity, and an unnecessary biblical literalism. In fact Darwin was reacting not against mainstream Christianity as we would understand it today but against a particular variety of fundamentalism which happened to be prevalent in his time and place.

Some of Darwin's contemporaries were able to reconcile the theory of evolution with their view of Christianity. The clergyman and writer Charles Kingsley wove a morality of evolution into a popular children's tale, *The Water-Babies,* which achieved classic status. He developed the idea that we have a choice between evolutionary progress and regress. Progress and survival depend on moral qualities such as determination and industriousness, operating not for the human species as a whole but as a discriminator between groups:

it is the individual's evolutionary duty to behave like a 'decent Englishman'.

Tragically, however, evolutionary principles were taken elsewhere to an extreme conclusion, dropping any pretence of compatibility with Christianity. Ernst Haeckel became well known across Europe and in the United States as the champion of a new religion of evolution that he called 'monism'.[13] Heinrich von Treitschke used the idea of the survival of the fittest to support nationalist and racist philosophy: only the brave would survive, and the weak would justly perish.[14] The conflicts between nations were part of the evolutionary process. Science justified racism and warfare. Today it is still common for the theory of evolution to be regarded as justifying an anti-Christian stance: this is the position generally taken by those who see modern science as a replacement for all religions.[15]

A different response to Darwinism is to reject it utterly on the grounds that it contradicts the literal word of the Bible. Biblical literalism has had a long and complex history as a strand within Christianity, and in some periods it has been more popular or more acceptable than in others; but it is fair to say that it has never been mainstream Christianity. What John Eriugena had to say about it in the ninth century illustrates that it was not universally accepted then:

> The authority of Holy Scripture must in all things be followed because the truth dwells there as though in a retreat of its own, but it is not to be believed as a book which always uses verbs and nouns in their proper sense... it employs certain allegories and transfers in various ways the meanings of the verbs and nouns out of condescension towards our weakness and to encourage by uncomplicated doctrine our senses which are still untrained and childish.[16]

Nevertheless 'creationism', or biblical 'fundamentalism', taking the Bible in opposition to the theory of evolution, is still a common stance in many parts of the world, and shows little sign of weakening.

Yet another response to Darwinism is 'epistemological dualism'. It is a very common attitude in mainstream Christianity and has acquired a certain intellectual respectability although it is basically erroneous. It holds that science and religion are independent of one another, deal with separate areas of knowledge, and address totally different questions. This view was adopted by John Henry Newman, the Victorian churchman and theologian. He wrote that knowledge must be divided into natural and supernatural, that science and theology cannot communicate with each other, so there are no grounds either for agreement or disagreement.[17] It has roots in late-medieval Aristotelian cosmology which saw the universe divided by a sphere of fire between sublunar (natural) and superlunar (supernatural) regions, which were quite different subjects of study. Newman's case is that physics deals only with the examination of cause and effect: it may resolve the complexity of phenomena into simple elements, principles and laws, but there its mission ends. It keeps within the material system, and never ventures beyond the fires which divide the earth from the heavens, the *flammantia moenia mundi*. So, since the theory of evolution is a scientific theory, it cannot contradict religion. The dualist can say that the theory of evolution may be valid within its own sphere, but that it is illogical to draw from it any conclusions of a theological or moral character. The theory of evolution, therefore, whether it be true or false, is said to be simply irrelevant to religion.

The final response to Darwinism, to which we now turn, is to accept the theory of evolution as a facet of a much grander scheme of cosmic evolution equivalent to the Christian vision of a transcendent destiny for all humanity and for the universe.

COSMIC EVOLUTION

The idea of cosmic evolution is not a strictly 'scientific' response to Darwin's theory: it breaches Newman's *flammantia moenia mundi*, the imagined boundary between science and religion. The idea has been expressed in different ways by different people using different vocabularies, but Pierre Teilhard de Chardin was one of its outstanding twentieth-century exponents. He imagined the whole of creation participating in a process of continuing evolution, which at the biological level eventually produced human beings. This introduced the phenomenon of conscious thought, so that evolution now operated at the global level of ideas, in a 'noosphere', which was superimposed on the 'biosphere'. Teilhard held that every physical being is endowed with an inner consciousness in proportion to its material complexity. There is an essential difference between this idea of human evolution and the kind of racist and therefore anti-Christian evolutionary religion mentioned earlier, where biological evolution is continuing, and is seen in the struggle for survival between races and nations. In the Teilhardian vision humanity has been united by Christ and biological evolution has given way to a collective mental evolution embracing all peoples.

Many other writers have considered that evolution, or something like it, proceeds at the level of shared ideas which develop and compete with one another in an abstract sphere which is somehow greater than the sum of the individual human minds which contribute to it. Even John Henry Newman, not normally regarded as an evolutionist, was putting forward in 1845 an essentially evolutionary theory of the development of Christian doctrine, describing how an idea can take on a life of its own, compete with other ideas, and prosper or die.[18]

The philosopher Karl Popper[19] put forward a similar view in which evolution has proceeded at three distinct and successive levels: biological, or genetic, evolution which gave rise to the the human species; behavioural evolution, involving social and technological development; and scientific evolution, taking place at the level of ideas. Purely genetic evolution 'by natural selection' long ago ceased to be significant for human progress, and human evolution today takes place most importantly on the higher plane of ideas. This is similar to Teilhard's idea of a noosphere.

More recently the case for evolution operating on a mental or scientific plane, in a hierarchical fashion, has been supported by writers such as the philosopher Michael Polanyi[20] and the theologian John Haught.[21] At the same time such ideas have had their opponents: for example Stephen Toulmin has criticised Teilhard de Chardin in particular on the grounds that his universalist ideas linking religion with biology and palaeontology are 'not scientific theories, but rather the current instalments in ... the tradition of "natural theology"'.[22] Toulmin sees Teilhard reverting to the pre-Darwinian position, not taking account of the full scientific implications of evolution, and being 'as much an amateur in theology as he was in evolutionary theory'.[23]

But Toulmin's criticism is unfair. Natural theology holds that human intelligence can prove the creator's existence with certainty through his works.[24] But in fact Teilhard and his followers go further than this, seeing the development of human wisdom not merely as a way of perceiving God, as the telescope allows us to perceive the stars, but as being the actual process of divinisation itself. Science, then, has intrinsic cosmic significance: it is at centre-stage, part of the opera, and not merely a better pair of opera-glasses. Science, or knowledge, is an aspect of salvation; in other words, as Jesus said, 'You will learn the truth, and the truth will set you free'.[25]

EVOLUTION, TENSION AND SIN

The idea of evolution provides a helpful new insight into the faults that are apparent in humanity's everyday behaviour and the predisposition that we seem to have towards evils of all kinds. This is what is traditionally known as original sin, sinfulness rooted in human origins. It is a concept that has often proved difficult to understand and justify. Many people find it an unhelpful and rather embarrassing strand of Christian tradition. Matthew Fox, a well-known proponent of creation spirituality, reacted against it with a recent book whose title, *Original Blessing,* is a deliberate inversion of original sin.[26] On the other hand Carl Jung took the extreme view that

> the evil that comes to light in man, and undoubtedly dwells within him, is of gigantic proportions so that for the Church to talk of original sin and to trace it back to Adam's relatively innocent slip-up with Eve is almost a euphemism. The case is far greater and is grossly understated.[27]

We can now understand this aspect of the human moral condition differently. We evolved to suit a social environment different from that in which we now find ourselves. Indeed, it could not be otherwise. The process of evolution in a changing environment necessarily implies a tension, an ill-fittedness between what we are and where we are. What we are is a reflection of all the past history of the chain of species that preceded us. But we live in the present, on the edge of the future. In the light of the theory of evolution we understand original sin in terms of the distressing tension that necessarily accompanies the continuing re-creation of humanity. As Teilhard de Chardin expressed it, the Fall of Adam from Eden 'cannot be located at one given moment of time or one given place', and is 'an aspect or global modality of evolution'. He expands on this issue:

> Physical and moral disorder, of one sort or another, must necessarily be produced spontaneously in a system which is developing its organic character, so long as the system is incompletely organised... From this point of view original sin, considered in its cosmic basis ... tends to be indistinguishable from the sheer mechanism of creation...[28]

THE CREATIVE COSMOS

The Teilhardian vision of cosmic evolution does not apply merely to humanity and to the Earth. Teilhard's final consummation, the Omega Point, which is also John Eriugena's final division of nature,[29] can be interpreted in the context of contemporary cosmology as coincident with the end-point or 'final singularity' of the universe as a whole.[30]

It is fundamental that the whole cosmos takes part in the creative process, even hypothetical intelligent life that might exist elsewhere in the universe. Teilhard has occasionally been misrepresented on this point,[31] but in fact he faced squarely the question of the plurality of inhabited worlds.[32] He concluded that there must be 'millions of human races dotted all over the heavens' but that 'the fundamental situation is still unchanged for the Christian in as much as he can regard these millions as reinforcing and glorifying the same unity as before'. Teilhard warns us against human-centredness, or an earth-centredness like that corrected by Copernicus in the sixteenth century: for Teilhard, Christ is 'universalised'.

IRREPRESSIBLE LIFE

The theory of evolution is scientifically secure and is based on what has been observed and understood of the irrepressible rise of life in the environment around us; and an appreciation of the fitness and fruitfulness of nature has always been central to the spirituality of creation. The evolutionary principle is to be appreciated positively as part of any complete and consistent philosophy of creation. Moreover, many of those who have taken evolution seriously have been drawn beyond mere biology towards the grander and more comprehensive vision, 'cosmic evolution'. This does not yet have the status of a single agreed theory and it tends to be associated with the faintly disreputable fringes of science and theology, but it has attracted some of the leading thinkers of the twentieth century. How far one goes down this road is a matter of personal choice, but it is an authentic and fulfilling part of the tradition of creation spirituality, which like any living tradition we ourselves must recreate in the light of our own times.

11

The web of life:
Reconnecting with the
sacred cosmos

EILEEN CONN

As we have seen through the eyes of some of our predecessors, the world can be experienced as a living, interconnected whole. And yet, for the last three hundred years the most influential idea in western society has been that of the machine. We have grown up in a world where life and spirit have mostly been separated off into the 'arts'. So 'modern art' reflects well the fractured soul-lessness of the economic and commercial machine which dominates the planet.

Not all the arts failed to be carriers of the ideas of life. Poets for example, like William Blake, were well aware that Newtonian science was not the complete explanation of the universe. His was a more holistic vision:

> To see a world in a grain of sand
> and a heaven in a wild flower,
> Hold infinity in the palm of your hand
> and eternity in an hour.
> ('Auguries of Innocence')

But modern scientists themselves have shown the limitations of the mechanistic approach. The great physicists of the modern age, such as Einstein and Heisenberg, have led us into understanding the relativity and uncertainty of space, time and matter. The recent development of chaos theory, made possible only through the help of computers, the ultimate product of the machine age, shows us what we, like Hildegard, intuitively knew, that there are astonishing patterns underlying the chaotic complexity of everything.

Darwin's discoveries about the relationships between different species and their common origins confirm our feelings about being part of the great web of life. The scientific theory of living systems, originating in cybernetics, is bringing together the ideas about the way that web of life works. New science and technology have enabled us to reconnect with the wholeness and vibrancy of the universe, and to continue our journey of exploration of our place in it, as humans with an awakened consciousness.

This has been accompanied by a significant shift in human awareness caused by seeing our planet Earth, our home, from space. One of the first astronauts described it as 'a blue and white globe floating in the deep darkness of space'.[1] This image has gone deep into the minds and hearts of millions of people, forever transforming their experience of their place in the web of life.

DEEP ECUMENISM

Religion is the main social institution which has carried the meaning of human experience from generation to generation throughout human history. Religious institutions and doctrines are therefore in a close, and often tense, relationship with the contemporary culture's scientific understanding. The development of scientific ideas will initiate turbulence for religions, as we have seen, for example, in the responses to Galileo and Darwin.

The religious expression of spirituality is now undergoing a change to match the shift from mechanistic science to holistic science. The image of the God out there, a remote male judge, an external creator, is developing into the God everywhere, intrinsic to life, an image more in tune with the new physics. This is closer to the thoughts of the sages and saints of our book, particularly of Eriugena, than to the machine age. But changing images in religions is difficult. Some people leave their churches or are expelled, while others are able to stay and develop new forms of worship and ritual which celebrate our late twentieth-century reconnection with the web of life.

There is also a great spiritual searching across the world in response to the impact of twentieth-century economics and industry. The collapse of communism, the rampant commercialism growing in its place, and the globalisation of industry and of the financial system, have left a trail of social and environmental damage in their wake throughout the world. Mechanistic and reductionist ideas, part of the rationalist approach, have played a large part in this in both communist and capitalist cultures. But as Vaclav Havel, the Czech president, has said, they have produced a 'mass insanity that has nothing in common with any form of rationality'.[2]

Some spiritual searching is being expressed by a retreat into fundamentalism in all religions, and into new religious movements, as people seek security and certainty in the face of severe damage to their environment, their cultures and themselves. But there is a different ferment within the mainstream religious world, reflecting the growing awareness of the wholeness and unity of the human race and our vital relationships with everything else in our biosphere on our planetary home. Over the last decade, leaders of world religions have been coming together to call for deep understanding between religions, to respond to the multiple global crises.[3]

Throughout the world these religious developments are matched by individual commitment to inter-faith relationships, respecting our differences while acknowledging our common humanity. Within Christianity there is increasing 'post-denominational' activity transcending the historical differences between sects. There is also a longing for a deeper ecumenism, touching that deep underground river from which all human spirituality springs. On the fringes, inside and outside the churches, Christians are developing a spirituality which reaches out and welcomes the diversity in religious faiths, seeing in diversity a sign of the richness and goodness of God's creation as Aquinas saw it so long ago.

There is a growing interest in cultural and spiritual roots worldwide. To be reminded of the way many of our predecessors in European Christianity understood their spirituality shows us that what may seem 'new' developments – expressing a belief in the sacredness and unity of creation – are in many ways a return to earlier Christian and Celtic ideas. The recovery of those traditions is vital to us in the social and environmental crises facing humanity as a whole. Because these old ways have been suppressed or have faded into obscurity, some in the west turn towards other religions. They are often unaware that their own Christian heritage shares much with the deeper teachings of other world faiths, and of native traditions.

But religion is just the exoteric, outer, expression of the esoteric, inner, experience of life, of spirit. The religious institutions are the holding structure, and the spirit is the life-flow, the breath of life; so there is natural tension between them, and sometimes conflict. The vital work for inter-faith understanding, the external expression, needs to spring from individual inner spiritual work.

THE INNER LIFE

In the last few decades there have been many significant developments in psychology, medicine and social sciences in understanding the human psyche and its effect on behaviour. This is leading to a holistic approach to the relationship between mind, body and spirit which Hildegard of Bingen would have found familiar in many respects.

These developments have accompanied the new ideas in physics, which are changing our understanding of the relationships between things. New physics encourages us to think more fluidly, and to grasp that simple mechanical cause and effect is very often inappropriate as a means of understanding life. The observer is part of what is observed. What happens in our individual outer life is affected by how we are in our inner self, and vice versa. This is of course a spiritual insight too, as Eckhart well knew; we need to dwell on finding the divine spark in us, and not confuse it with external material things. Practising radical detachment and letting-go while living fully in the material world is an ancient spiritual discipline in accord with modern psychology.

This might be seen as discovering our unconscious self, what it is that motivates us both positively and negatively. Life is a mixture of joy and suffering in our engagement with the world, and each of us will experience it differently. It is a journey, so well described by Dante, and the more conscious we are of this the more we will develop a creative way of learning from our experiences, both the positive and negative ones. To do this we need to be in touch with our whole selves, body and soul.

Our brains and minds are stimulated by all our physical senses, our full incarnation in the body. Thinking and feeling are inseparable. In our industrialised society we have to a large extent lost the joy of being in touch with all our senses. They need to be used in harmony to enable us to have a full, holistic experience. Many of us have lost the art of just being. We have become compulsive 'doers'. We need to savour nature again, experience it as an integral part of our lives, be part of it, and not just visit it for the day. We can also reawaken our intuitive and creative senses with such things as poetry, drama, music, painting, sculpture, dance. They belong to us all, not just to specialists, and need to be reintegrated into our lifelong education to balance rational, logical and analytical training.

INNER BEING — OUTER DOING

We are social beings: as individuals we experience life not only in our interactions with our physical environment, but also in our relationships with other humans and other creatures. How we are within ourselves affects the nature and quality of these relationships, through which our actions have their effects. So, as exemplified by Cuthbert of Lindisfarne, the quality of our individual inner spiritual life affects the quality of the communal spirit.

There is a communal spirit in every grouping of humans who join together to do something, whether this is as a family, as a group of friends, or as a work group. It is mainly through groups that we act to affect the world. Teilhard de Chardin recognised the significance of this in his ideas about the noosphere, involving the evolution of humanity to a new level of communion, of shared consciousness with each other and our environment. For Teilhard this was a psychosocial development, one which would enable us to act corporately beyond the sum of the powers of the individuals, just as previous evolutionary stages have involved simpler organisms joining forces to form more complex organisms.

Our unconscious motives get in the way of clear communication with others, and prevent the effective joining together which Teilhard foresaw as a possibility. New developments in psychology are enabling increasing numbers of individuals to understand themselves at this deeper level, and to discover their true vocations.[4] We can use these insights to improve our relationships when we act together. Otherwise we will continue to act out our unconscious motives, and all our unhealed wounds from life experiences, within the groups to which we belong. Herein lies one of the sources of what Teilhard called 'moral disorder', the inevitable accompaniment of social evolutionary change, from the suffering in everyday life to the terrible acts of evil perpetrated in political, religious and ethnic conflicts.

The suffering is increased by the disorder passed on through the generations, which then becomes systemic.[5] This is seen most obviously where violent conflicts have their roots many generations ago, but it is also true of much of the social disorder in 'normal' societies. We, as individuals and communities, need to heal the deep wounds which bring about these evils and disorders. To do this we need to face the void, as Dante did on his journey into hell. But this can be deeply terrifying, and we need help and support on the journey. This was often the traditional role of the clergy. Today it is vital work to which many people increasingly contribute.[6] When this work is successful, it springs from an understanding of the qualities of love and compassion. Nurturing these, and acknowledging our common humanity and frailties, are powerful ways of strengthening our sense of interconnectedness and respect for each other. They are qualities which were well understood by Cuthbert of Lindisfarne and Julian of Norwich, and they are vital to the achievement of effective relationships and good community. Our difficulties and our differences can be seen positively as gifts to help us grow, instead of being sources of conflict. We can share Thomas Aquinas' delight in the diversity of God's creation as we discover more about the important and creative role which differences play in the web of life, both in human psychology and in ecology.

THE CHANGING WORLD

Some of these new insights are already understood by some people within large corporations who are exploring how they can be applied to modern commercial life. In the rapid changes in technology and markets which are being experienced today, it is a common understanding in business that only those companies which are successful in learning how to adapt quickly will succeed. The 'learning organisation' is thought to be essential to survival, an idea which rests in part on ideas about personal and spiritual development and the growth of true community.[7] The spiritual ideas of the mystics and sages are emerging in the apparently soul-less commercial world.

If people like Teilhard are right in their views about cosmic and human evolution, then we could expect there to be a timely confluence of ideas at this critical point in human history. And indeed there is. There are an increasing number of initiatives worldwide which recognise the interdependence of mainstream business with all the key groups with which they interact, including their shareholders, their employees, their suppliers, their customers, the local communities affected by their activities, and the impact of their operations on the natural environment.[8] This is a welcome recognition of the reality of the web of life, especially as our way of business is at the heart of the machine age.

There is also a worldwide growth in holistic and organic practices. They can be found in the social, economic, commercial, environmental and political walks of life, in the local, national and global spheres.[9] Spurred on by a multitude of grassroots initiatives, the ideas are spreading to mainstream organisations.

But the dominant attitudes in government, the professions and commerce are still materialistic and mechanistic. People are still seen as a 'labour cost' to be reduced or dispensed with. Machines are seen as replacements for people, not as extensions of human skills. Business relationships with customers and local communities are still often about minimising cost or contact. The natural environment is still a resource to be plundered for profit maximisation. Nothing could be further from the Franciscan vision that we are related to the whole of creation. This is particularly stark in the agricultural world. Satisfaction of the most basic human need (for food) has been turned into a massive chemical and engineering industry, with an almost complete divorce of many western people from the source of what they eat each day. Food itself is increasingly artificial and of questionable nutritional value, produced at tremendous cost to the whole ecological system. The environment is polluted, our fellow creatures suffer painful lives, farm workers have poor conditions, and people's land is adversely affected, especially in the 'Third World'. That term itself illustrates the attitude of dualism, 'us and them'. The 'Third World' feeds the great machine of the 'First World'. We prevent ourselves from seeing the earth as one world.

Mechanistic attitudes lie behind the management of basic public services, for example, in health and education. The means has in practice long obscured the ends. In health, the high-technology approach of drugs and surgery, while providing welcome benefits in certain situations, has dominated medicine to the detriment of real health; treating the person as only a body to be repaired has led to escalating costs and has lost sight of the whole living person who is mind and spirit as well as body. In education, the technique of the factory, of an assembly line of products to be processed at lowest cost, has too often replaced the activities needed to nurture young and growing humans. Part of the consequence is a growing alienation of the young, a loss of the idea of vocation, and an increase in violence and lawlessness.

Thomas Hardy poignantly portrays the human sense of loss that developed in the nineteenth century – the loss of certainty, of innocence, of spiritual connection with creation. However he also delights in a wonder which he saw in nature. There is a reaching out for a new relationship with the natural world. But sadly, the alienation felt then has now been exacerbated by the loss of purpose in a society created by market economics. Humans have become consumers, and are dispensable in the production process. This is the logical development of the machine culture, and a complete inversion of the place of humans as part of the sacred web of life. Work in providing for ourselves, and celebrating life, is an integral aspect of being human. Yet 'work' today is more about tending the great economic machine which now straddles the planet. Without authentic work, humans cannot be whole. Our individual and collective cosmic sin is in failing to face up to the consequences of our actions. But there is another way.

BRINGING FORTH A WORLD

We are all part of creating the world in which we live. Each one of us is responsible for our own actions. Our images of ourselves and our lives can fundamentally change our individual and collective experience. As Matthew Fox writes 'During the Newtonian Age, we not only thought we lived in a machine, we behaved accordingly. If we think we live in an interconnected universe, an organism unfolding ... in motion and expanding, we will start living in such a world as well'.[10]

Such a change has been evolving for many decades. Increasing numbers of people across the world are now thinking of the universe as a living, interconnected whole. They are exploring themselves, and their own relationships with the world around them, in a new way. This underlies the worldwide growth in holistic and organic initiatives. These survive and grow in spite of the obstacles of a machine dominated age. We create the world as we see it in our minds, and as we feel it in our relationships. Living systems science is beginning to show how this works.[11] The renewal of the vision of creation as a magnificent, organic whole, the renewal of our collective and individual spiritual consciousness, can 'bring forth a world', a new world. Reconnecting with the sacred cosmology of the past, the holistic visions of our ancestors, helps each one of us to nurture the roots of the whole tree of life.

Notes, references and further reading

PROLOGUE: VISIONS OF LIFE

1 Fritjof Capra, 'The Theory of Living Systems', in *Elmwood Quarterly*, (The Elmwood Institute, Berkley, CA.) 1993 (Spring/Summer), p7ff; 'Bringing Forth a World', ibid., 1993 (Fall), p4ff, and 'Shiva's Dance Revisited', ibid., 1993-1994 (Winter), p14ff. See also Capra, F., *The Turning Point: Science, Society, and the Rising Culture*, Fontana Paperbacks, London, 1983.

2 J. Bronowski, *The Ascent of Man*, BBC Books, London, 1976, ch.7.

3 Descartes, *Philosophical Writings*, selected and translated by Elizabeth Anscombe and Peter Thomas Geach, Nelson, London, 1954, p229ff.

4 *Ibid*. pp20, 23. See also the Third Meditation: 'Concerning God: That he Exists', pp76ff.

5 Bronowski, *op. cit.*, pp196-218.

6 T.W. Rolleston, *Myths and Legends of the Celtic Race*, Constable, London, 1986: pp127-145 include discussion of the female deities of the Celts and their meanings. Ch.V. covers the Ulster Cycle and legends of Cuchulain.

7 Bertram Colgrave, *Two Lives of Saint Cuthbert*, Cambridge University Press, 1985: pp231-239, 263, 265, 273 give hints of the Celtic abbesses' relationships with Cuthbert. Bede, *History of the English Church and People*, Penguin Books, 1956: pp240ff. give the Life of St Hilda of Whitby.

8 Simeon, *A History of the Church of Durham*, Llanerch Press, Lampeter, facsimile, 1988. Pp65-66, 86 indicate some of the changes regarding women and marriage in the Church.

9 Revelations 22.1-2.

10 Proverbs 28.18.

Further reading

Ronald Bainton, *The Penguin History of Christianity*, Volumes 1 and 2, Penguin Books.

J. Bronowski, *The Ascent of Man*, BBC Books, London, 1973.

Fritjof Capra, *The Turning Point: Science and the Rising Culture*, Fontana

Paperbacks, London, 1985.

Gordon Leff, *Medieval Thought: St. Augustine to Ockham*, Pelican Books.

'Milestones of History' series, Volumes *2, The Fires of Faith 312-1204; 3, Expanding Horizons 1415-1516*; and *4, Reform and Revolt 1517-1600*. Each volume is illustrated with colour plates. Weidenfeld and Nicolson, New York, for Newsweek Books.

James Bruce Ross and Mary Martin McLaughlin, *The Portable Medieval Reader, Extracts from medieval letters and documents*, Viking Press, NY, 1975. The introduction is particularly useful.

Ross Thomson, *Holy Ground: The Spirituality of Matter*, SPCK, London, 1990.

1 COMPASSION AND COMMUNITY: CUTHBERT OF LINDISFARNE

1 We have several sources for the life of St Cuthbert. *The Anonymous Life* was written on Lindisfarne soon after his death by a member of his own community between AD 698-705. Bede's *Prose Life* took material from the *Anonymous Life* and added further stories from witnesses, around AD 721. Bede's *History of the English Church and People*, completed at Jarrow in 731, gives a further outline in the context of other events, and a full account of the Synod of Whitby (ch.IV. 26-32.). Simeon's *History of the Church of Durham*, written in 1096, gives a medieval view of Cuthbert which shows how his image had been changed to suit the attitudes of the later church (chs.IV-XI). It also outlines the history of the Community of St Cuthbert up to the coming of the Norman bishops. Cuthbert now rests beneath a slab of polished stone behind the high altar of Durham Cathedral, identified by one word inlaid in brass letters: CVTHBERTVS.

2 W.F.H. Nicolaisen, *Scottish Place Names*, Batsford, London 1976, ch.5.

3 T.W. Rolleston, *Myths and Legends of the Celtic Race*, Constable, London, 1985. Reprint paperback edition p83.

4 R. Van deWeyer, *Celtic Fire; an anthology of Celtic Christian Literature*, Darton, Longman and Todd, London, 1990, p70. Also C. Bamford and W.P. Marsh, *Celtic Christianity, Ecology and Holiness*, Floris Classics, Edinburgh, 1986, p112.

5 B. Bainton, *The Penguin History of Christianity, Vol.I*, Penguin Books, Harmondsworth, 1964, ch.5.

6 Bede's *A History of the English Church and People*, ch.I 22-29, ch.I 33-II.3 outline Augustine's arrival and ministry, including the problems he had with the British churches, and his correspondence with Pope Gregory.

7 Bede, *Prose Life*, ch. XXXIX.

8 *Ibid.*, ch. XXIII.

Further reading

David Adam, *Fire of the North: The Illustrated Life of St Cuthbert*, SPCK, London, 1993.

S. Baring-Gould, *Lives of the Northumbrian Saints*, Llanerch Press, Lampeter, 1990.

Bede, *A History of the English Church and People*, translated by Leo Sherley-Price, Penguin Classics, London.

Bertram Colgrave, *Two Lives of Saint Cuthbert*, Cambridge University Press, paperback edition, 1985.

Simeon, *A History of the Church of Durham*, Llanerch Press, Lampeter, 1988.

Shirley Toulson, *The Celtic Alternative: A Reminder of the Christianity We Lost*, Rider, London, 1987.

Ann Warin, *Hilda: An Anglo-Saxon Chronicle*, Lamp Press, London, 1989.

2 A CELTIC COSMOLOGY: REDISCOVERING JOHN ERIUGENA

1   See J. J. O'Meara, *Eriugena*, Oxford University Press, 1988.

2   Eriugena, *Periphyseon*, revised translation by J. J. O'Meara, Bellarmin, Montreal, 1987, Book V, 925A.

3   *Periphyseon*, Book I, 489C.

4   Attributed to the druid Amergin, translated by Thomas Kinsella, *New Oxford Book of Irish Verse*, Oxford University Press, 1989.

5   Quoted by J. Ferguson in *Pelagius: A Historical and Theological Study*, W. Heffer and Sons, Cambridge (England), 1956, p37.

6   *Periphyseon*, Book IV, 768B.

7   *Periphyseon*, Book III, 650A.

8   Eriugena, *Commentary on St.John's Gospel*, quoted by H. Bett in *Johannes Scotus Erigena: A Study in Mediaeval Philosophy*, Cambridge University Press, Cambridge, 1925, pp9-10.

9   *Periphyseon, op. cit.*

10 *Periphyseon*, Book V, 927C.

11 *Periphyseon*, Book I, 455C.

Further reading

Christopher Bamford, *The Voice of the Eagle: The Heart of Celtic Christianity*, Floris Books, Edinburgh, 1990.

J.J. O'Meara, *Eriugena*, Oxford University Press, Oxford, 1988.

See also passages indexed under Eriugena in Gordon Leff, *Medieval Thought: St Augustine to Ockham*, Pelican Books.

3 THE INTERCONNECTED UNIVERSE:
HILDEGARD OF BINGEN

1 A detailed list of Hildegard's major works can be found in Bowie and Davies (editors), *Hildegard of Bingen: An Anthology*, SPCK, London, 1990. This short book is a readable and rounded introduction to Hildegard's life and works.

2 The contemporary and near contemporary biographies are important sources for material about Hildegard's life. Gottfried completed the first volume of *Vita Sanctae Hildegardis* before he died in 1176, and volumes 2 and 3 were completed by Theodoric within a few years of her death. Guibert also wrote a biography. These biographies include some auto-biographical material written by Hildegard. Other extant writings of Hildegard about herself include her extensive correspondence and the prefaces to her visionary books. Details for these sources can be found in Sabina Flanagan, *Hildegard of Bingen: A Visionary Life*, Routledge, London and New York, 1989, pp226, 227.

3 *Scivias*, translated by Hart & Bishop, introduction by Barbara Newman, Paulist Press, New York, 1990, p59. (Declaration)

4 Some of these paintings are reproduced in *Illuminations of Hildegard of Bingen*, with commentary by Matthew Fox, Bear & Co., Santa Fe, 1985.

5 See for example the accounts in Flanagan, *op. cit.*, pp199-213.

6 For a useful discussion on Hildegard's place in Christian doctrinal history and spiritual tradition, see the introduction by Barbara Newman to *Scivias, op. cit.*

7 *Book of Divine Works*, edited and introduced by Matthew Fox, Bear & Co., Santa Fe, 1987, p86. V4, 11. This book also contains selected letters and songs.

8 *Ibid.*, p10. V2.

9 *Ibid.*, p97. V4, 21

10 *Scivias, op. cit.*, p120. I. V4, 16.

11 *Divine Works, op. cit.*, p206. V8, 2.

12 *Scivias, op. cit.*, p255. II. V6, 28.

13 *Divine Works, op. cit.*, p38. V2,18.

14 *Scivias, op. cit.*, p475. III. V10, 4.

15 Gabrielle Uhlein, *Meditations with Hildegard of Bingen*, Bear & Co., Santa Fe, 1983, p41.

16 *Divine Works, op. cit.*, p26. V2, 2.

17 *Ibid.*, 2, 3, 4.

18 *Ibid.*, p41. V2, 24.

19 *Ibid.*, p171. V5, 15.

20 *Ibid.*, p45. V2, 32.

21 *Ibid.*, p90. V4, 14.

22 James Gleick, *Chaos: Making a New Science*, Sphere, London, 1989.

23 *Divine Works, op. cit.*, p35. V2, 15.
24 *Ibid.*, p63. V3, 2.
25 *Ibid.*, p101. V4, 24.
26 *Ibid.*, p74. V3, 15.
27 *Ibid.*, p82. V4, 2.
28 *Scivias, op. cit.*, p335. III. V2, 19.
29 *Divine Works, op. cit.*, p44. V2, 29.
30 *Ibid.*, p53. V2, 46.
31 *Ibid.*, p37. V2, 18.
32 *Ibid.*, p340. Letters.
33 *Ibid.*, p340. Letters.
34 *Scivias, op. cit.*, p153. II. V1, 8.
35 *Divine Works, op. cit.*, p359. Letters.
36 Original paintings, produced around 1165 under Hildegard's personal supervision at St Rupertsberg, survived until the twentieth century but were lost in the Second World War. Fortunately, a hand-copied and hand-painted facsimile had been produced in 1927-1933 by the nuns at Eibingen Abbey (the surviving convent from Hildegard's foundation). This gives us access to the original colours and designs as seen by Hildegard. Some of them are reproduced in *Illuminations of Hildegard of Bingen, op. cit.*
37 She gathered the songs together towards the end of her life as the *Symphonia* (The Symphony of the Harmony of Heavenly Revelations). She also developed the last vision of *Scivias* into an opera 'Ordo Virtutum' (The Play of Virtues), considered to be the first morality play.
38 *Scivias, op. cit.*, p. 534. III. V13, 14.
39 Available on cassette: *A Feather on the Breath of God: Sequences and Hymns by Abbess Hildegard of Bingen.* Sung by Gothic Voices, directed by Christopher Page, Hyperion, London, 1982. There is also an increasing number of public performances of her music.
40 *Divine Works, op. cit.*, p357. Letters.

Further reading

Bowie and Davies, (editors), *Hildegard of Bingen: An Anthology*, Translations by Robert Carver, SPCK, London, 1990.

Hildegard of Bingen, *Scivias*, (translated by Columba Hart and Jane Bishop, Introduction by Barbara Newman), Classics of Western Spirituality, Paulist Press, New York, 1990.

Sabina Flanagan, *Hildegard of Bingen: A Visionary Life*, Routledge, London and New York, 1989.

Matthew Fox, (editor), *Hildegard of Bingen's Book of Divine Works with Letters and Songs*, Bear & Co., Santa Fe, 1985.

Matthew Fox, *Illuminations of Hildegard of Bingen*, Bear & Co., Santa Fe, 1985.

Gabrielle Uhlein, *Meditations with Hildegard of Bingen*, Bear & Co., Santa Fe, 1983.

4 KINSHIP WITH NATURE: FRANCIS OF ASSISI

1 *The Canticle of the Sun* as quoted in this chapter is from *Celebrating Common Prayer*, Society of St Francis, Mowbray, Bath Press, 1992, p232.
2 Thomas of Celano, adapted from Murray Bodo, *Through the Year with St Francis*, Fount Paperbacks, London, 1988.
3 St Mark 16, 15.
4 R.D. Sorrell, *St. Francis of Assisi and Nature*, Oxford University Press, New York, 1988, pp92, 94.
5 *Ibid.*, p94.

Further reading

Julian Green, *God's Fool*, Hodder & Stoughton, London, 1986.
Brother Ramon, *Franciscan Spirituality*, SPCK, London, 1994.
Roger D. Sorrell, *St Francis of Assisi and Nature*, Oxford University Press, New York, 1988.

5 THE MEANINGS AND VALUES OF CREATION: THOMAS AQUINAS

1 For a detailed look at Thomas' life and teaching, see the works by Chesterton, Tugwell, and listed in Further reading.
2 Leo J. Elders, S.V.D., *The Philosophical Theology of St Thomas Aquinas*, E. J. Brill, Leiden, 1990, pp282-83. For a brief history of philosophical treatments of creation, see pp277-85.
3 *Quaestiones disputatae: De Potentia*, Tomus II, q.3, a.3, Marietti Ed., Turin, 1949, p43. English translation by Thomas Gilby, O.P.
4 *Summa Theologiae*, Ia, Q.45, A.1.
5 *Introduction to Metaphysics* [1953], trans. by Ralph Manheim, Anchor, Garden City, 1961, p1.
6 For a penetrating examination of Thomas' teaching on the unity of the universe and its implications for modern physical science, see the article by Stanley Jaki in Further reading.
7 Elders, *op.cit.*, pp308-09.
8 *De Potentia*, III, 17.
9 *De Potentia*, III, 14 ad 8.
10 *Summa T.*, Ia, Q.46, A1 ad 8.
11 *Summa T.*, Ia, Q.46, A.1.
12 Tugwell, p228.
13 *Summa T.*, Ia, Q.47, A.1. Emphasis added.
14 *Summa T.*, Ia, Q.47, A.2, ad 1.
15 Tugwell, pp212-213, says: 'For Thomas, it is not really the marvellous

complexity and ingenuity of things that alerts the mind to the reality of God, it is rather the metaphysical implications of very simple observations about things, beginning with the primary fact of their being there at all... The immediate connection ... between existence and God is implicit in much of this theology, because it underlies his deep conviction that there can never be any separation between God and his creatures... The fact that things exist and act in their own right is the most telling indication that God is existing and acting in them. Without this ... Thomas would never have developed his doctrines of creation and providence and grace'.

16 Carolyn Merchant, *The Death of Nature: Women, Ecology, and the Scientific Revolution*, Harper and Row, San Francisco, 1990, p193.

17 Edward Conze, *Buddhist Meditation*, Unwin, London, 1956, pp19-20.

18 *Summa Contra Gentes*, III, 69, translated by Gilby.

19 *Summa T.*, IIa-IIae, Q.76. A.2, translated by Gilby.

20 The writings of John Barrow and other scientists with regard to the 'cosmic-anthropic principle' supports such a vision from a fully scientific perspective. And whatever else may eventuate in the centuries ahead, at present, for all practical purposes such as observation, measurement, and even physical exploration, the universe remains as geocentric as it was in the days of Thomas Aquinas and Columbus. Planet Earth is the only home we have.

Further reading

G.K. Chesterton, *St. Thomas Aquinas*, Sheed and Ward, New York, 1933.

Brian Davies OP, *The Thought of Thomas Aquinas*, Clarendon Press, Oxford, 1992.

Leo J. Elders SVD, *The Philosophical Theology of St Thomas Aquinas*, E.J. Brill, Leiden, 1990.

Matthew Fox, *Sheer Joy*, Harper Collins, San Francisco, 1992.

Stanley L. Jaki, 'Thomas and the Universe', in *The Thomist*, 53, 4 1989: 545-72.

Simon Tugwell (editor), *Albert and Thomas – Selected Writings*, Paulist Press, New York, 1988.

William A. Wallace O.P., 'Aquinas on Creation: Science, Theology, and Matters of Fact', in *The Thomist*, 38 1974: 485-523.

6 REDISCOVERING WISDOM: MEISTER ECKHART

1   M. O'C. Walshe, *Meister Eckhart: Sermons and Treatises*, Element Books, Shaftesbury, 1987, Sermon 56, p81.

2   *Ibid.*, S84, p258.

3   *Ibid.*, S67, p151.

4   *Ibid.*, S69, p165.

5   *Ibid.*, S57, p85.

6 *Ibid.*, S31, p229.
7 *Ibid.*, S69, p165.
8 *Ibid.*, S13B, pp117ff.
9 Colledge & McGinn, translators & editors, *Meister Eckhart: The Essential Sermons, Commentaries, Treatises & Defence*, Paulist Press, New York, 1981, p265.
10 Walshe, *op. cit.*, S4, p39.
11 Colledge & McGinn, *op. cit.*, p220.
12 Walshe, *op. cit.*, S4, p44.
13 Walshe, *op. cit.*, S7, p67.
14 Walshe, *op. cit.*, S9, p87.
15 Walshe, *op. cit.*, S65, p135.
16 Walshe, *op. cit.*, vol. 111, p46.
17 Walshe, *op. cit.*, S37, p270.
18 Walshe, *op. cit.*, S56, p82.

Further reading

Ursula Fleming (editor), *Meister Eckhart: The Man From Whom God Hid Nothing*, Fount Paperbacks, London, 1988.

Matthew Fox, *Breakthrough: Meister Eckhart's Creation Spirituality*, new translation, Image Books, New York, 1980.

Jeanne Ancelet-Hustache, *Master Eckhart and the Rhineland Mystics*, Longman, Green and Co., London, 1957.

Cyprian Smith, *The Way of Paradox*, Darton, Longman and Todd, London, 1987.

Anne Wilson-Shaef, *When Society Becomes An Addict*, Harper and Row, San Francisco, 1988.

M. O'C. Walshe, *Meister Eckhart Sermons and Treatises*, Vols I, II and III, Element Books, Shaftesbury, 1987.

Richard Woods, *Eckhart's Way*, Darton Longman and Todd, London, 1987.

7 THE SOUL'S JOURNEY – THE DIVINE COMEDY: DANTE ALIGHIERI

1 See Dante's *Convivio*.
2 Dorothy Sayers, (trans.), *Dante: The Divine Comedy: Hell*, Penguin Books, 1980, Introduction, p11.
3 Jean Hardy, *A Psychology with a Soul*, Penguin, 1989.
4 Helen Luke, *Dark Wood to White Rose: a study of meanings in Dante's Divine Comedy*, Dove Publications, New Mexico, 1975.
5 *Hell, op. cit.*, Canto XXXIV, lines 108-111.
6 *Hell, op. cit.*, Canto XXXIV, line 120.
7 Helen Luke, *op. cit.*, p9.
8 Dorothy Sayers (trans.), Dante: *The Divine Comedy: Purgatory*, Penguin

Penguin Books, 1981, Introduction, p17.

9   *Purgatory, op. cit.,* Canto II, lines 122-3.

10 *Purgatory, op. cit.,* Canto XXX, lines 32-3.

11 *Purgatory, op. cit.,* Introduction p16.

12 Dorothy Sayers and Barbara Reynolds, (trans.), *Dante: The Divine Comedy: Paradise,* Penguin Books, 1982, Canto XXVII, lines 106-9.

13 *Paradise, op. cit.,* Canto XXX, line 63.

14 *Paradise, op. cit.,* Canto XXXIII, lines 142-5.

15 Helen Luke, *op. cit.,* p116.

16 Allan Hunt Badiner (editor), *Dharma Gaia,* Parallex Press, Berkeley, 1990. See chapter by Joanna Macy, 'The Greening of the Self'.

17 Joanna Macy, *World as Lover, World as Self,* Parallex Press, Berkeley, 1991, p12.

18 T.S. Eliot, 'Burnt Norton', part IV.

19 W.Wordsworth, 'Ode; Intimations of Immortality from Recollections of Early Childhood'.

20 *Hell, op. cit.,* Introduction, p27.

Further reading

Dorothy Sayers (translator), *Dante: The Divine Comedy: Hell,* Penguin Books, London, 1980.

Dorothy Sayers (translator), *Dante: The Divine Comedy: Purgatory,* Penguin Books, London, 1981.

Dorothy Sayers and Barbara Reynolds (translators), *Dante: The Divine Comedy: Paradise,* Penguin Books, London, 1982.

Jean Hardy, *A Psychology with a Soul,* Penguin Books, London, 1989.

Helen Luke, *Dark Wood to White Rose: A Study of Meanings in Dante's Divine Comedy,* Dove Publications, New Mexico, 1975.

Joanna Macy, *World as Lover, World as Self,* Parallex Press, Berkeley, 1991.

8 A PERSPECTIVE ON LOVE: JULIAN OF NORWICH

All references are to *Julian of Norwich: Showings, (Short and Long Text),* translated and edited by Edmund Colledge OSA. and James Walsh SJ, Paulist Press, New York and Mahwah, New Jersey, 1978.

1   p125.

2   p177.

3   p135.

4   p259.

5   p266.

6   p336.

7   p135.

8   p273.

9   *ibid.*

10 pp295-296.
11 p293.
12 p190.
13 *ibid.*
14 p199.
15 p186.
16 pp288-289.
17 p279.
18 p183.
19 p314.
20 p246.
21 p186.
22 *ibid.*
23 p225.
24 p342.

Further reading

Julian of Norwich, *Revelations of Divine Love*, translated and introduced by Clifton Walters, Penguin Books, London, 1966.

Julian of Norwich, *Showings, (Short and Long Text)*, Edmund Colledge OSA and James Walsh SJ (translators and editors), Paulist Press, New York and Mahwah, New Jersey, 1978.

Members of the the Julian Shrine (compilers and translators), *Enfolded in Love*, Darton, Longman and Todd, London, 1980.

Brendan Doyle (editor), *Meditations with Julian of Norwich*, Bear & Co., Santa Fe, 1983.

Gloria Durka, *Praying with Julian of Norwich*, Saint Mary's Press, Winona, Minn., 1989.

Grace Jantzen, *Julian of Norwich*, SPCK, London, 1992.

Robert LLewelyn (editor), *Julian, Woman of our Day*, Darton, Longman and Todd, London, 1985.

9 THE POET AS MYSTIC: THOMAS HARDY

1 George Herbert, 1593-1633. His poetry was published posthumously under the title *The Temple: Sacred Poems and Private Ejaculations*.
2 Gerard Manley Hopkins, 1844-1889. Most of his poems were published posthumously. The first collected edition was in 1918.
3 *Jude the Obscure*, Macmillan, 1895.
4 Benjamin Britten, 1913-1976. There are a number of recordings of this cycle of songs including one on the Decca label with Peter Pears and Benjamin Britten.
5 T.S. Eliot, 1888-1965.
6 *Tess of the d'Urbervilles*, Macmillan, p449.

7   Hardy, *Complete Poems*, Macmillan, p534.
8   Charles Darwin, 1809-1882. He laid the foundation of modern evolu-
    tionary theory with his concept of the development of all forms of life
    through the slow-working process of natural selection. See *On the
    Origin of Species*, 1859. See also Chapter 10 below.
9   Edmund Gosse, 1844-1928, *Father and Son*, Penguin Classics, London.
10 Matthew Arnold, 1822-1888.
11 'Dover Beach', 1867. This poem can be found in many anthologies
    including *The New Oxford Book of English Verse*, edited by Helen
    Gardner, Oxford University Press, p703.
12 'The Oxen', in *Complete Poems*, p468; also in *The New Oxford Book of
    English Verse*, p769.
13 'Proud Songsters', in *Complete Poems*, p835.
14 This tendency towards disorder in the natural world has long puzzled
    scientists who lacked the mathematical means to deal with chaotic
    systems. Recent developments in the study of Chaos Theory, particu-
    larly by the American physicist Mitchell Feigenbaum, have determined
    certain consistent patterns within the seeming disorder making Hardy's
    thinking appear curiously modern here.
15 'Wagtail and Baby', in *Complete Poems*, p296.
16 'The Darkling Thrush', in *Complete Poems*, p150; also in *The New
    Oxford Book of English Verse*, p757. Note particularly the end of the
    poem

> ...I could think there trembled through
> His happy good-night air
> Some blessed Hope, whereof he knew
> And I was unaware.

17 'Before Life and After', in *Complete Poems*, p277.
18 'At the Railway Station, Upway', in *Complete Poems*, p607.
19 'A Philosophical Fantasy', in *Complete Poems*, p894.

Further reading

James Gibson (editor), *Complete Poems of Thomas Hardy*. Macmillan,
    London, 1976.
Robert Gittings, *Young Thomas Hardy*, Penguin, London, 1978.
James Reeves and Robert Gittings (editors), *Selected Poems of Thomas Hardy*,
    Heinemann, Oxford, 1981.

10 THE EVOLVING CREATION:
CHARLES DARWIN AND
PIERRE TEILHARD DE CHARDIN

1   See Pierre Teilhard de Chardin, *Christianity and Evolution*, (trans. René
    Hague), Collins, London, 1971; and Charles E. Raven, *Teilhard de
    Chardin Scientist and Seer*, Collins, London, 1962.

2 See Adrian Desmond and James Moore, *Darwin*, Michael Joseph, London, 1991.
3 Charles Darwin, *On the Origin of Species by Means of Natural Selection, or The Preservation of Favoured Races in the Struggle for Life*, Watts and Co., London, 1950, p410.
4 Charles Darwin, *op.cit.*, pp413-414.
5 *Ibid.*, p163.
6 Psalm 8.
7 Alfred Lord Tennyson, 'In Memoriam, LXI,' in *The Works of Alfred Lord Tennyson*, Macmilllan, London, 1902.
8 Gerard Manley Hopkins, 'Nondum', in *Poems and Prose*, Penguin, 1953.
9 Matthew Arnold, 'Dover Beach', in F.T. Palgrave and C. Day Lewis (editors), *The Golden Treasury*, Collins, London, 1954. See also Chapter 9 above.
10 See Colin Russell, *Cross Currents: Interactions between Science and Faith*, Inter-Varsity Press, Leicester, 1985.
11 Charles Darwin, *The Autobiography*, edited by Nora Barlow, Collins, London, 1958, p85.
12 *Ibid.*, p87.
13 Ernest Haeckel, *Les Enigmes de l'Univers*, Schleicher Frères, Paris, ca.1900.
14 Heinrich von Treitschke, quoted by D.R. Oldroyd, in *Darwinian Impacts*, Open University Press, Milton Keynes, 1980, p217.
15 E.g. Peter Atkins, *The Creation*, W.H. Freeman, Oxford, 1981.
16 John Eriugena, *Periphyseon*, translated by John J. O'Meara, Bellarmin, Montréal, 1987, 509A.
17 John Henry Newman, *The Idea of a University*, edited by Ian Ker, Fontana, Oxford, 1983 pp78-86.
18 John Henry Newman, *Essay on the Development of Christian Doctrine*, quoted by Ian Ker in *Newman the Theologian*, Collins, London, 1990.
19 Karl Popper, *Evolutionary Epistemology*, in *A Pocket Popper*, edited by David Miller, Fontana, Oxford, 1983. pp78-86.
20 Michael Polanyi, *Personal Knowledge: Towards a Post-Critical Philosophy*, Routledge and Kegan Paul, London, 1973, p388.
21 John Haught, *'The Cosmic Adventure,'* Paulist Press, New York, 1984.
22 Stephen Toulmin, *The Return to Cosmology: Postmodern Science and the Theory of Nature*, University of California Press, 1985, p123.
23 *Ibid.*
24 *Catechism of the Catholic Church*, 286, Geoffrey Chapman, London, 1994.
25 St John 8.32.
26 Matthew Fox, *Original Blessing*, Bear and Co., Santa Fe, 1983.
27 Carl Jung, quoted in *Towards a Story of the Earth: Essays in the Theology of Creation*, Denis Carroll, Dominican Publications, Dublin, 1987, p90.

28 Pierre Teilhard de Chardin, *Christianity and Evolution*, (trans. Hague), *op. cit.*, pp149–150.

29 See Chapter 2 above.

30 John D. Barrow and Frank J. Tipler, *The Anthropic Cosmological Principle*, Oxford University Press, Oxford, 1988, p195ff.

31 Toulmin, *op. cit.*, pp125–126; and Barrow and Tipler, *op. cit.*, p203.

32 Pierre Teilhard de Chardin (trans. Hague), *op. cit*, p229ff.

Further reading

Matthew Fox, *Original Blessing*, Bear & Co., Santa Fe, 1983.

Blanche Gallagher, *Meditations with Teilhard de Chardin*, Bear & Co., Santa Fe.

Sean P. Kealy, *Science and the Bible*, Columba Press, Dublin, 1987.

Thomas King SJ and Mary Wood Gilbert (editors), *The Letters of Teilhard de Chardin and Lucile Swan*, Georgetown University Press, 1994.

Ursula King, *The Spirit of One Earth, Reflections on Teilhard de Chardin and Global Spirituality*, Paragon House, New York, 1989.

Mary Midgely, *Evolution as a Religion: Strange Hopes and Stranger Fears*, Methuen, London, 1985.

11 THE WEB OF LIFE: RECONNECTING WITH THE SACRED COSMOS

1 Cited in Fritjof Capra, 'The Theory of Living Systems', in *Elmwood Quarterly*, Spring/Summer, 1993, p7. (The Elmwood Institute, 2522 San Pablo Ave, Berkeley, CA.).

2 Vaclav Havel in 'Living in Truth', cited in Matthew Fox, *The Reinvention of Work; A New Vision of Livelihood for Our Time*, HarperCollins, San Francisco, 1994, p49.

3 For example in 1986 in Assisi, world religious leaders agreed on the need for urgent action on the environmental crises. In 1993, in Chicago, the centenary meeting of the first World Parliament of Religions launched 'The Declaration of a Global Ethic'. This affirmed that a common set of core values is to be found in the teachings of all the religions; that these form the basis of a global ethic based on the interdependence of all life; and that all of us need to take responsibility for our actions. See also Hans Küng, *Global Responsibility: In Search of a New World Ethic*, SCM Press, London, 1991.

4 For example psychosynthesis, amongst many other approaches. See also M. Scott Peck, *The Road Less Travelled; A New Psychology of Love, Traditional Values and Spiritual Growth*, Century Hutchinson, London, 1983.

5 A stimulating contribution to the research into these systemic disorders is David Wasdell's paper, *Psychodynamics of War and Religion*, URCHIN, (Meridian House, 115 Poplar High Street, London E14 0AE), 1991.

Also now published as *Die pränatalen und perinatalen Würzeln von Religion und Krieg*, Centaurus Verlag, Pfaffenweiler, Germany, 1993.

6   This work includes personal and spiritual development; different counselling and psychotherapy approaches; a wide variety of work on group processes; skilled mediation to resolve conflicts in all kinds of situations. Some approaches are at early stages; some are controversial; many are contributing to the vital healing work of increasing our understanding of ourselves, individually and collectively.

7   See for example Peter Senge, *The Fifth Discipline; The Art and Practice of The Learning Organisation*, Century Business, London, 1993.

8   See for example, *Tomorrow's Company: The Role of Business in a Changing World, Interim Report: the case for the inclusive approach*, Royal Society of Arts, (8 John Adam St, London WC2N 6EZ), 1994. Also Adams, Carruthers & Hamil, *Changing Corporate Values*, Kogan Page, London, 1991.

9   Many towns now have focal points for information about such initiatives, for example: centres for natural and holistic health, for personal and spiritual growth, for community business and new economics projects, and for environmental projects.

10 Matthew Fox, *The Reinvention of Work; A New Vision of Livelihood for Our Time*, HarperCollins, San Francisco, 1994, p75.

11 According to the Santiago theory of cognition, developed by Chilean scientists Maturana and Varela, a living system interacts with its environment in a way which triggers structural change in the system itself. A significant aspect of this is that the living system not only specifies what these structural changes will be, but also which patterns in its environment will trigger them. By doing this, the system itself 'brings forth a world'. Fritjof Capra argues that this is a scientific theory which unifies mind, matter and life. (*Elmwood Quarterly, ibid.*, Fall 1993, p5). It also indicates how humanity, as a living system, can 'bring forth its own world'.

Further reading

Paul Davies, *God and the New Physics*, Penguin, London, 1983.

Matthew Fox, *The Reinvention of Work: A New Vision of Livelihood for Our Time*, HarperCollins, San Francisco, 1994.

Al Gore, *Earth in the Balance: Ecology and the Human Spirit*, Houghton Mifflin, Boston, 1992.

James Gleick, *Chaos: Making a New Science*, Cardinal, London, 1988.

Patricia Hedges, *Understanding Your Personality*, SPCK, London, 1993.

E.F. Schumacher, *Small is Beautiful; A Study of Economics as if People Mattered*, Sphere, London, 1974.

M. Scott Peck, *The Different Drum; The Creation of True Community*, Random Century, London, 1988.

FURTHER INFORMATION

Readers interested in following up the ideas touched on in this book may write to The Association for Creation Spirituality (ACS), c/o St. James's Church, 197 Piccadilly, London, W1V OLL.

ACS coordinates a network of local activities throughout the UK, including a mail order book and tape service, workshops, talks, study groups and publications.

There are also leaflets for individuals or groups interested in exploring or studying the ideas in this book in more depth.

Any other comments or responses to this book may be addressed to the editors, care of the Association for Creation Spitituality at the above address.